N. Dubois Miller

Competency of witnesses in civil causes in Pennsylvania as affected

by legislation,

With especial reference to the act of April 15, 1869

N. Dubois Miller

Competency of witnesses in civil causes in Pennsylvania as affected by legislation,
With especial reference to the act of April 15, 1869

ISBN/EAN: 9783337724474

Printed in Europe, USA, Canada, Australia, Japan

Cover: Foto ©ninafisch / pixelio.de

More available books at **www.hansebooks.com**

THE COMPETENCY OF WITNESSES

IN

CIVIL CAUSES IN PENNSYLVANIA

AS AFFECTED BY LEGISLATION,

WITH ESPECIAL REFERENCE TO

THE ACT OF APRIL 15, 1869.

By N. DUBOIS MILLER,
Of the Philadelphia Bar.

PHILADELPHIA:
REES WELSH & CO.
1881.

Entered according to Act of Congress
By REES WELSH & CO., 1881.

PREFATORY NOTE.

IN this State, indeed throughout the United States, that branch of evidence which relates to the competency of witnesses is passing through a transition period. We have partly broken away from the old rules, but have not yet cut loose from them, and the result is, that while a knowledge of the old law is not less important than it was before, there has grown up in addition to the recent statutes, and dependent upon them, a very considerable body of law, the principles of which it is incumbent upon the practitioner to know; but they can only be discovered by the careful study of numerous decisions, and those withal not free from difficulty. In view of this, it seemed possible, that an attempt to collect and arrange the cases in this State, so that the principles settled by them might be the more readily discovered and understood, would prove useful. As to the scheme upon which the work has been done, it is enough to say, that if the book is to have any value at all, it should be as a book of easy and ready reference. For this purpose the historical treatment seemed at once the easiest to comprehend and the simplest in arrangement; the cross-references have been made numerous, and the index and citations from the authorities very full; to each case decided since 1865 there has been added the date on which the opinion was delivered.

I have ventured to differ with the reasoning upon some of the decisions, and to suggest irreconcilable differences between others. I can only hope that the views expressed may not prove to be erroneous.

N. D. M.

216 SOUTH FOURTH STREET, November 9th, 1881.

TABLE OF CONTENTS.

PART I.—THE COMMON LAW OF THE STATE RELATING TO THE INCOMPETENCY OF WITNESSES.
PART II.—LEGISLATION AND ITS RESULTS.

PART I.

THE COMMON LAW OF THE STATE.

CHAPTER I.—THE INCOMPETENCY OF WITNESSES.

	PAGE
Incompetency of witnesses, definition,	17
Incompetent testimony, definition,	17
Incompetent witnesses,	18
General incompetency,	18
Special incompetency,	19

CHAPTER II.—INCOMPETENCY ARISING FROM INTEREST.

Interested persons. Definition of interest, it must be,	20
Pecuniary,	21
Legal,	21
Certain,	22
Immediate,	22
In the result of the issue,	23
Interest in the result of the issue,	23
a. His liability for costs, or,	23
b. A fund in which he will be legally entitled to share, and which will be created, enlarged, or diminished by the result of the suit,	25
(1.) Inhabitants of a borough, township, or city,	25
(2.) Members of a private corporation, or unincorporated society and partners,	26

CONTENTS.

	PAGE
(3.) Debtors or creditors of one of the parties,	27
(4.) Assignors entitled to a surplus of the fund or property,	28
(5.) Heirs and legatees,	29
Interest in the record as an instrument of evidence,	29
(*a.*) To shift the burden of all or part of a debt from the witness,	30
(*b.*) To exonerate from a secondary liability,	33
(*c.*) Where the record may be used by the witness to sustain a claim,	35
(*d.*) To fix liability upon him when not *prima facie* responsible,	35
(*e.*) Where the judgment may serve to charge the estate of the witness or deprive him of it,	37
Interest in equilibrio,	38
Preponderance of interest,	38
Testimony against interest,	39

CHAPTER III.—EXCEPTIONS TO THE RULE OF EXCLUSION ON ACCOUNT OF INTEREST.

1. To prove collateral facts for the information of the court,	41
2. *Ex necessitate rei*,	43
3. Agents,	44
4. Trustees and members of charitable or religious societies,	46
Privilege of refusing to testify,	46

CHAPTER IV.—HISTORY OF RELEASES.

Removal of disqualification by release,	48

CHAPTER V.—WAIVER OF PRIVILEGE AND REMOVAL OF DISABILITY BY RELEASE.

Waiver of privilege and disqualification,	56
The removal of disabilities,	57
What constitutes a good release,	59

CHAPTER VI.—PRACTICE.

Matters of practice,	60
(1.) The time of the objection,	60
(2.) Method of bringing the objection before the court,	61
(3.) Character of the objection,	63
(4.) Other matters of practice,	64

PART II.

LEGISLATION AND ITS RESULTS.

CHAPTER I.—EARLY LEGISLATION.

	PAGE
Tendency of Judiciary and Legislature,	69
Earlier Acts of Assembly,	70

CHAPTER II.—THE ACTS OF 1865 AND 1867.

The Acts of March 27th, 1865,	73
Relating to executors,	73
Adverse parties,	74
1. Subsequent competency,	75
2. Credibility lost by death of party calling,	77
Definition of an "adverse party," etc.,	79
Acts of March 28th and April 10th, 1867,	81
Legislation elsewhere,	82

CHAPTER III.—THE ACTS OF APRIL 15TH, 1869, AND APRIL 9TH, 1870.

Section 1 of the Act of April 15th, 1869,	85
The Act of April 9th, 1870,	85
"No interest nor policy of law" defined,	88

CHAPTER IV.—THE FIRST CLAUSE OF THE PROVISO.

Husband and wife competent for each other,	92
(1.) The effect to be given to the testimony of husband or wife for the other,	93
(2.) What is interest against husband or wife,	94
(3.) Testimony of husband or wife for or against the estate of the other,	96
(4.) Confidential communications,	97
Counsel and client,	98

CHAPTER V.—THE SECOND CLAUSE OF THE PROVISO.

Meaning of "actions,"	99
Actions by or against executors or administrators,	101

(1.) The settlement of estates in the Orphans' Court,	102
(2.) Suits at common law or in equity,	103
(a.) When the witness is a party to the record,	103
(b.) When the witness offered is not a party to the record,	104
Actions by or against guardians,	106
(1.) Where the assignor of the thing or contract in action may be dead,	107
First. Definition of the thing or contract in action,	113
Second. The method of assignment,	114
Third. The extent to which the exclusion operates,	115
(2.) The "assignor" must have been beneficially interested,	121
(3.) The mere fact of having been a party to a transaction with the deceased assignor no ground for exclusion,	123
(4.) All parties on both sides incompetent,	124
The case of husband and wife under the proviso,	126
The case of infamous persons under the proviso,	130

CHAPTER VI.—THE ACT OF APRIL 9TH, 1870, AND THE EXCEPTION TO THE PROVISO OF THE ACT OF 1869.

The Act of April 9th, 1870,	131
Testimony of any facts existing subsequent to the death of the "assignor," etc., competent,	131
The exception to the proviso,	133

CHAPTER VII.—THE SECOND AND THIRD SECTIONS OF THE ACT OF APRIL 15TH, 1869.

The second section,	138
(1.) Who may be called under this section,	139
(2.) Application of this section to divorce proceedings,	140
(3.) The application of this section to cases not within the enabling clause,	141
(4.) The degree of credibility conferred by calling a witness under the second section,	142
(5.) The credibility of co-plaintiffs or co-defendants of parties called under the second section,	143
The third section,	143
Its use in connection with the second section,	143
(1.) Notes of testimony or depositions in subsequent trials,	144
(2.) The admission of the deposition or notes of previous testimony of one of the parties does not render the adverse party competent,	147

(3.) Admissibility on his own behalf of notes of testimony or deposition of witness called by the adverse party for cross-examination, ... 148

Chapter VIII.—Subsequent Legislation.

The Act of March 4th, 1870, ... 151
    Unsupported testimony of either party sufficient, ... 151
    Competency of the surviving party, ... 152
    The act purely an enabling one, ... 153
The Act of June 8th, 1874, ... 153
The Act of May 25th, 1878, ... 154
    Definition of "partners," 154
The Act of May 11th, 1881, ... 155

Chapter IX.—General Results of the Legislation.

The Act of April 15th, 1869, an enabling act, ... 156
The credibility of witnesses rendered competent by statute, . . . 157
Parties to the record, as such no longer excluded, ... 159
Releases, ... 161
The effect upon other rules of evidence, ... 163
Matters of practice, ... 164
    Previous admissions of party, ... 164
    Continuance on account of absence of party, ... 164
    Cross-examination of a party testifying on his own behalf, . . . 164

ACTS OF ASSEMBLY.

	PAGE		PAGE
1705, ———,	70	1865, March 27th. Executors, etc.,	73–4, 157
1718, May 31st,	70		
1788, October 4th,	70	1867, March 28th,	81, 157, 159
1794, April 3d,	70	1867, April 10th,	81, 143, 157
1799, April 11th,	71	1869, April 10th, 84–150, 151, 153, 154	
1832, March 29th,	71		155, 156–164
1840, February 19th,	71	1870, March 4th,	141, 151
1840, April 16th,	71	1870, April 9th,	85, 107, 130, 131
1851, April 15th,	122	1874, June 8th,	153, 157
1854, May 8th,	71	1878, May 25th,	154
1860, March 31st,	19	1881, May 11th,	104, 130, 131, 155
1865, March 27th. Adverse Parties,	73–81, 138–9, 143, 148, 161		

UNITED STATES AND BRITISH STATUTES.

	PAGE		PAGE
Act of Congress, 1864, July 2,	83	14 and 15 Victoria,	82
9 and 10 Victoria,	83		

(xi)

TABLE OF CASES.

	PAGE
Adams Co., Thornbury v.,	71
Agnew v. Whitney,	106
Ahl, Foreman v.,	53
Albert, Given v.,	51
Alexander, Plumer v.,	35, 45
Allen, Comm. v.,	36, 45
Allum v. Carroll,	78, 81, 103
Alsop, City v.,	127
American Iron Co., O'Connor v.,	76
Ammon, Malaun's Admr. v.,	52
Anderson v. Young's Exrs.,	63
Anspach, Bast v.,	92
Appleton v. Donaldson,	54
Armstrong v. Graham,	53, 60, 62
Himblewright v.,	55
Pattison v.,	117, 120
Railroad Co. v.,	35, 45
Armstrong Co., Rhoads v.,	24, 25
Arthurs v. King et al.,	111
Asay v. Hoover,	58
Asch v. R. W. Co.,	144
Ash v. Guie,	79, 154, 157, 161
Ash v. Patton,	42, 50, 64
Atkinson v. Purdy,	39
Avery, Post v.,	50
Bache, Dodge v.,	35, 36, 46
Bacher, Wash. Ben. Soc. v.,	46
Bailie, Long v.,	22
Baily v. Knapp,	52
Baird v. Cochran,	40
Baird, Comm. v.,	25
Ballentine v. White,	93, 158
Bank, Batdorf v.,	64
v. Beale,	45
v. Beck,	40
v. Brown,	42, 59
v. Downing,	65
v. Forster,	54
v. Green,	26
v. Hadfeg,	41
Irvine v.,	22, 26
Jones v.,	40
London S. F. S. v.,	35, 45, 53, 56
v. McCalmont,	54
Meighen v.,	57
v. Rhoads,	89, 90
Shoemaker v.,	57

	PAGE
Bank, Thompson v.,	54
v. Walker,	54
Whitehead v.,	56
v. Wikoff,	61
v. Wood,	40
Banks v. Clegg,	63
Baring v. Shippen,	55
Barnet v. School Directors,	71
Barr, Davis v.,	62
Barton v. Fetherolf,	55
Bast v. Anspach,	92
Batchelder, Wolf v.,	76
Batdorff v. Bank,	64
Baxter v. Graham,	37
Beale, Bank v.,	45
Beale, Hoopes v.,	104
Beaver v. Beaver,	53
Beck, Bank v.,	40
Beneficial Society v. Comm.,	26, 46
Beidelman v. Foulk,	33
Bennett v. Hethington,	21, 37
v. Williams,	76
Bennett's Estate,	98
Bennett's Exrs., Speyerer & Co. v.,	146
Bickham v. Smith,	64
Bierly's Appeal,	65, 102, 129, 143
Bingham, Mifflin v.,	62
Bingham v. Rogers,	44
Bird, Parke v.,	51
Bird v. Smith,	33
Bisbing v. Graham,	54
Bixler, Clement v.,	50
Black v. Marvin,	59
v. Moore,	43
Blackstone v. Leidy,	62
Blantz's Estate,	102
Blewett v. Coleman,	38
Bobst, Marshall v.,	64
Bodey, Saurman's Exr. v.,	54
Boileau, Vansant v.,	23
Bomberger, Kreiter v.,	164
Bovard, Floyd v.,	75
Bovard, Simpson's Exr. v.,	160
Bowen v. Burk,	40, 56
Bowen v. Goranflo,	134
Bowers, Gordon v.,	62, 63
Boyer v. Kendall,	27
v. Smith,	36

(xiii)

TABLE OF CASES.

	PAGE
Boyle v. Haughey,	97
Brady v. Reed,	112, 118, 119
Brady, Thomas v.,	63
Braine v. Spalding,	46
Bray, Rex v.,	69
Breban, Evans v.,	61
Breitenbach v. Houtz,	37
Brendel, Craig v.,	93, 116, 119, 120, 127, 159, 163
Breneman's Estate,	65, 72, 100, 102
Brenneman, Kifer v.,	37
Brewer v. Kaughley,	42
Brewster's Admr. v. Sterrett,	47
Brice v. Shultz,	164
Bright, Carey v.,	29
Brindle v. McIlvaine,	38
Bronson v. Bronson,	81, 140, 153
Bronson, Hawthorn v.,	40
Brown, Bank v.,	42, 59
v. Burk,	40
v. Downing,	33, 54
Entriken v,	32
v. Parkinson,	28
Ralph v.,	40, 47
Browne v. Weir,	50
Brownfield, Jones v.,	27
Brubaker v. Taylor,	139, 164
Bruner v. Wallace,	40, 162
Buchanan v. Buchanan,	29
v. Montgomery,	59
Shields v.,	33, 34
v. Streper,	41, 157
Buck, Robinson v.,	61, 64
Bull, Snyder v.,	22
Burbridge, Keymborg v.,	36
Burd, Potter v.,	38
Burk, Bowen v.,	40, 56
Brown v.,	40, 56
Burrows v. Shultz,	51
Bye, Roberts v.,	34
Byers v. Mullen,	27, 59
Cambria Iron Co. v. Tomb,	52
Cameron v. Paul,	59
Camp v. Stark,	134
Campbell, Rooney v.,	52
Cannell v. Crawford Co.,	71
Carey v. Bright,	29
Carothers, Wolf v.,	40
Carroll, Allum v.,	78, 81, 103
Carskadden v. Poorman,	41
Cassel, Hepburn v.,	54
Cassiday v. McKenzie,	22
Cartledge, Stranbridge v.,	36
Catanach, Strawbridge v.,	111
Cawley v. Wilson,	92, 131
Chase v. Irvin's Exrs.,	103, 112
Chase v. Goldsborough,	61, 62
Childs, Leib v,	32
Christman v. Siegfried,	37

	PAGE
Church, Dickinson Coll. v.,	24, 36, 59
City v. Alsop,	127
Clark, Frew v.,	134
Clark, Shaffer v.,	158
Clark v. Spence,	44
Clarion Co., Wilson v.,	71
Cleavinger v. Rymar,	33
Clegg, Banks v.,	63
Clement v. Bixler,	50
Clover v. Painter,	53
Clyde v. Clyde,	55
Cochran, Baird v.,	40
Coleman, Blewett v.,	38
Comm. v. Allen,	36, 45
v. Baird,	25
Dorrance v.,	35, 45
Linton v.,	45
McFarland v.,	71
v. McKee's Exr.,	24
Marion Ben. Soc. v.,	26, 46
v. Railroad Co.,	57
Shannon v.,	62
v. Watmough,	59
Condron, Peters v.,	43
Congregation, Ryerss v.,	24
Conrad v. Conrad,	97
v. Keyser,	36
Conrow, Mitchell v.,	54
Conwell, McNeil v.,	36
Cook v. Grant,	58
Cooper, Jordan v.,	42
Welsh v.,	47
Copley, Schuylkill Co. v.,	18, 91
Cornell v. Vanartsdalen,	29, 58
County v. Leidy,	44
Cowan, Ben. Soc. v.,	26, 46
Cox v. McKean,	74
v. Norton,	58
Coxe v. Ewing,	42
Craig v. Brendel, 93, 116, 119, 120, 127, 159, 163	
Crall, McCormick v.,	42
Crane, Whitesell v.,	44
Crawford Co., Cannell v.,	71
Crissy, Roth v.,	59
Crouse v. Staley,	124, 129, 131, 156
Crozer v. Leland,	42
Culbertson v. Isett,	45
Cullum v. Wagstaff,	63, 64
Cummings, Richter v.,	74
Cunningham, Lecky v.,	74
Daniels et al., Lyon v,	62
Dannels v. Fitch,	35
Darlington's Appropriation,	40
Davenport v Freeman,	25, 39
David v. Moore,	44
Davies v. Morris,	46
Davis v. Barr,	62
v. Houston,	42

Davis, O'Brien v.,	54
Quinlan v.,	47, 56
Williams v.,	159, 163
Dayton v. Newman,	59
De Haas, Lenox Admr. v.,	41
Dela, Evans v.,	53, 54
Dellinger's Appeal,	127
Dellone v. Rehmer,	58
Dennis, Garwood v.,	43
Derrickson v. Wilbur,	97
Dickinson v. Dickinson,	39
Dickinson Coll. v. Church,	24, 36, 59
Diehl v. Emig,	43, 126, 131
Emig v.,	133, 147
Diffebach, Nav. Co. v.,	41
Dimond v. McDowell,	29
Dispensary, Wise v.,	144
Dobson, Ridgeley v.,	45
Dodge v. Bache,	35, 36, 46
Doebler v. Snavely,	33
Donaldson, Appleton v.,	54
Dornick v. Reichenback,	33
Dorrance v. Comm.,	35, 45
Dougherty, Malone v.,	165
Douglass, Wharton v.,	64
v. Sanderson,	42
Downer, Mulford v.,	157
Downing, Bank v.,	65
Downing, Brown v.,	33, 54
Drexel v. Man,	64
Dryden, Purviance v.,	32
Dundas v. Muhlenberg's Exrs.,	32
Dunlap v. Smith,	62
Duquesne, Prescott v.,	24
Dyer, McInroy v.,	61
Eichelberger, Hinkle v.,	36
Eichman, Kelly v.,	34
Eilbert v. Finkbeiner,	103
Eldridge, Robinson v.,	27, 35
Ely v. Hager,	22
Emig, Diehl v.,	43, 126, 131
v. Diehl,	133, 147
Enters v. Peres,	27
Entriken v. Brown,	32
Espy, Gest v.,	54
Ross v.,	65
Est. Amb. White,	42
Jac. Hyneman,	72
John Blantz,	102, 103, 142
Evans v. Breban,	61
v. Dela,	53, 54
v. Jenks's Ex.,	162
Evans's Admrx. v. Reed,	144, 146, 148
Ewing, Coxe v.,	42
v. Ewing,	113, 119, 120
Kirk v.,	51
Eyster, Menges v.,	77, 78, 149, 156
Faber, King v.,	40, 63
Fay, Patterson v.,	64
Faylc's Est.,	102
Fegley, Heckert v.,	32
Felton, Langer v.,	55
Ferree v. Thompson,	28, 123
Fetherolf, Barton v.,	55
Fetterman v. Plummer,	50
Fidelity Company's Appeal,	152
Finkbeiner, Eilbert v.,	103
Finks, Wolf v.,	51
Finney's Appeal,	28, 38
First German Cong., Sorg v.,	46
Fitch, Dannels v.,	35
Hickling v.,	31, 45
Flattery v. Flattery,	152, 158
Flickwire, Rush v.,	24, 39
Flora, Little's Lessee v.,	43
Floyd v. Bovard,	75
Foreman v. Ahl,	53
Forrester v. Kline,	58, 76, 77, 78, 150
Forsman, Wolfinger v.,	22
Forster, Bank v.,	54
Foster, Pitts. Coal Co. v,	63
Foulk, Beidelman v.,	33
Fox, Ins. Co. v.,	54
v. Lyon,	43
Frazier, Hill v.,	26, 31
Miller v.,	35, 37
Freeman, Davenport v.,	25, 39
Frew v. Clark,	134
Funk, Wright v.,	162
Galbraith v. Galbraith,	62
Gallagher v. Milligan,	24
Gallaher, Rothrock v.,	132, 147, 164
Gamble, Hepburn v.,	104
Gardner, Musser v.,	94, 96
Gardner v. McLallen,	110
Garsed v. Turner,	64
Garvin's Exr., Miller v.,	34
Garwood v Dennis,	43
Gavit v. Supplee,	111, 125
Geoghegan, Reid v.,	38
Gest v. Espy,	54
Gibb, McEwen v.,	50
Gibbs et al., Hogeboom's Exr. v.,	79, 105, 139
Gicker's Admr. v. Martin,	28
Gilchrist, McKee v.,	59
Gillespie v. Goddard,	64
Lessee of Pollock v.,	61
v. Miller,	27
Gilpin v. Howell,	46
Given v. Albert,	51
Goddard, Gillespie v.,	64
Goldsborough, Chase v.,	61, 62
Goodman v. Losey,	33
Goods, McVeaugh v.,	22
Gordon v. Bowers,	62, 63
Goranflo, Bowen v.,	134

TABLE OF CASES.

	PAGE
Gourley, Hess v.,	101, 112, 118, 124, 129
Graham, Armstrong v.,	53, 60, 62
Baxter v.,	37
Bisbing v.,	54
Graff, McCaskey v.,	27, 64
Grant, Cook v.,	58
v. Levan,	43
Montgomery v,	24, 58, 59
Graves v. Griffin,	53, 162
Gray, Zeigler v.,	38
Grayble v. Railroad Co.,	26
Grayson's Appeal,	52
Green, Bank v.,	26
Greenawalt v. McEnelly,	97, 136, 137
Greenwalt v. Horner,	33
Grier, Hayes v.,	33
Griffin, Graves v.,	53, 162
Griffith v. Reford,	54, 63
Gross v. Reddig,	94
Gudykunst, Hayes v.,	31, 40
Guie, Ash v.,	79, 154, 157, 161
Guldin v. Guldin,	39, 80, 139
Gyger's Appeal,	102
Hadfeg, Bank v.,	41
Hager, Ely v.,	22
Hagerman, Patterson v.,	47
Hanbest's Exrs., Sheetz v.,	123, 156
Hancock, McCormac v.,	40
Hanna v. Wray,	110, 154
Hansell v. Lutz,	31
Harbeson, Kisterbock v.,	126
Harding v. Mott,	54
Harley v. Perot,	60
Harris, Schuyl. Nav. Co. v.,	35, 45, 59
Hart v. Heilner,	50, 62, 63
Hartman v. Ins. Co.,	57
Morrison v.,	24, 39
Hartz v. Woods,	31
Hartzell, Steffen v.,	37
Hatz v. Snyder,	53
Haughey, Boyle v.,	97
Haus v. Palmer,	58
Hawthorn v. Bronson,	40
Hayes v. Grier,	33
v. Gudykunst,	31, 40
Hayman, Miller v.,	45
Haynes v. Hunsicker,	62, 63
Nichols v.,	163
Hay's Appeal,	146, 149
Heath, Steamboat Dictator v.,	61
Heckert v. Fegley,	32
Heenan, Lahey v.,	64
Heilner, Hart v.,	50, 62, 63
Henderson v. Lewis,	32
Taylor v.,	47
Hepburn v. Cassel,	54
v. Gamble,	104
Herdic, Waltman v.,	117, 120
Hethington, Bennett v.,	21, 37

	PAGE
Hess v. Gourley,	101, 112, 118, 124, 129
Hess, Stroh v.,	34
Hickling v. Fitch,	31, 45
Hickman, Railroad Co. v.,	26
Hill v. Frazier,	26, 31
Himblewright v. Armstrong,	55
Hinckley v. Waters,	34
Hinkle v. Eichelberger,	36
Hoak v. Hoak,	50
Hoch's Exr., Steininger v.,	58
Hoffman v. Strohecker,	24
Strohecker v.,	59
Hogeboom's Exr. v. Gibbs et al.,	79, 105, 139
Holmes, McGinn v.,	34
Hoopes v. Beale,	104
Hoover, Asay v.,	58
Hopple's Est.,	97, 136, 137
Horner, Greenwalt v.,	33
Horbach, Peters v.,	52, 56, 64
Hostetter v. Schalk,	122, 125, 126
Hottenstein's Appeal,	53
Houston, Davis v.,	42
Houtz, Breitenbach v.,	37
Howell, Gilpin v.,	45
Huff's Lessee, Vincent v.,	62, 63
Humphreys v. Reed,	36, 45
Hunsicker, Haynes v.,	62, 63
Huzzard, Trego v.,	63
Hyneman's Est.,	72, 103, 142
In re Darlington's Appropriation,	40
Samuel Knabb,	102
Innis v. Miller,	22
Ins. Co. v. Fox,	54
Hartman v.,	57
v. Ins. Co.,	26
Ludlow v.,	22, 37
v. Marr,	38
v. Shultz,	121, 156
v. Simmons,	59
Steele v.,	49, 50, 57, 163
Irvine v. Bank,	22, 26
Irvin's Exrs., Chase v.,	103, 112
Isett, Culbertson v.,	45
Iturbide's Est.,	72, 75, 103
Jackson v. Litch,	165
Jackson, Meeker v.,	43
Jacoby v. Laussat,	38
Jenks's Exrs., Evans v.,	162
Johns, U. S. v.,	26
Johnson, Railroad Co. v.,	50, 52
Johnston, Norris v.,	51, 58
Sennett v.,	64
Jones v. Bank,	40
v. Brownfield,	27
Martin v.,	32
v. Patterson,	31
v. Shawhan,	32

TABLE OF CASES.

xvii

	PAGE
Jones, Smull v.,	61
Jones's Appeal,	61
Jordaine v. Lashbrooke,	53
Jordan v. Cooper,	42
Kaine, Meason v.,	31, 45
Karne v. Tanner,	90, 107, 115, 122, 126, 162
Karsper v. Smith,	42
Kase, Work v.,	54
Kauffman v. Kauffman,	154
Kaughley v. Brewer,	42
Keck, Kuester v.,	37
Keever, Moddewell v.,	52, 56, 160
Keim v. Taylor,	24
Kelly v. Eichman,	34
Rick v.,	54
Taylor v.,	124, 128, 129
Kendall, Boyer v.,	27
Struthers v.,	45
Kennedy v. Phillipy,	32
Kerns v. Soxman,	58
Keymborg v. Burbridge,	36
Keyser, Conrad v.,	36
v. Rodgers,	43
Kidd v. Riddle,	42
Kifer v. Breneman,	37
Kimball v. Kimball,	29
King et al., Arthurs v.,	111
v. Faber,	40, 63
Kirk v. Ewing,	51
Kirkpatrick, Muirhead v.,	53
Kisterbock v. Harbeson,	126
Kitzmiller, Lilly v.,	59
Kline, Forrester v.,	58, 76, 77, 78, 150
Knabb, In re,	102
Knapp, Baily v.,	52
Kneass's Case,	44
Koehler, Schnable v.,	37
Krause v. Reigel,	34
Kreiter v. Bomberger,	164
Kronk v. Kronk,	55
Kuester v. Keck,	37
Lahey v. Heenan,	64
Laley, Noble v.,	52
Langer v. Felton,	55
Lanning, Patterson v.,	33
Lashbrooke, Jordaine v.,	53
Laubach v. Laubach,	64
Laussat, Jacoby v.,	38
Lantzerheiser, Sheerer v.,	35, 45
Lecky v. Cunningham,	74
Lee v. Welsh,	63
Leib v. Childs,	32
Leidig, Watts v.,	104, 116, 162
Leidy, Blackstone v.,	62
County v.,	44
Leis, Stub v.,	36
Leland, Crozer v.,	42

	PAGE
Lenox Admr. v. De Haas,	41
Lent, Rhodes v.,	32
Levan, Grant v.,	43
Levers v. Van Buskirk,	29, 37
Levy, Shaw v.,	42, 47
Lewis, Henderson v.,	32
Lilly v. Kitzmiller,	59
Lincoln v. Wright,	28
Lindsley v. Malone,	52
Linton v. Comm.,	45
Litch, Jackson v.,	165
Little's Lessee v. Flora,	43
Livingston, Rees v.,	22, 38, 61, 63
Lodge v. Patterson,	29
Long v. Bailie,	22
v. Long,	31
Sharp v.,	29
v. Spencer,	131
Utt v.,	32
Longswamp v. Trexler,	36
Losey, Goodman v.,	33
Lothrop v. Wightman,	27, 64
Loudon Sav. F. S. v. Bank,	35, 45, 53, 56
Loyd, Union Canal Co. v.,	42
Ludlow v. Ins. Co.,	22, 37
Ludwig, Myre v.,	59
Lutz, Hansell v.,	31
Lynch, Stille v.,	54
Lyon v. Daniels,	62
Lyon, Fox v.,	43
Lytle, Peiffer v.,	63
McBride's Appeal,	97, 99, 102
McCabe v. Morehead,	34
McCalmont, Bank v.,	54
McCaskey v. Graff,	27, 64
McClay, Work v.,	40
McClelland v. Mahon,	51
McClelland's Exr. v. West's Admr.,	161, 162
McClenachan, Miller v.,	32
McCord, Martin v.,	57
McCormac v. Hancock,	40
McCormick v. Crall,	42
McCulloch, Solms v.,	52, 56, 160
McDowell, Dimond v.,	29
v. Simpson,	45
McEnelly, Greenawalt v.,	97, 136, 137
McEwen v. Gibb,	50
McFarland v. Comm.,	71
McFerran v. Powers,	55
McFerren v. Mont Alto Iron Co.,	117, 156
McGeary's Appeal,	96
McGill v. Rowand,	44
McGinn v. Holmes,	34
McGrath, O'Rourke v.,	80, 140
McGunnagle v. Thornton,	45
McHugh, Rowley v.,	96

B

TABLE OF CASES.

Case	Page
McIldowney v. Williams,	55
McIlroy v. McIlroy,	58
McIlvaine, Brindle v.,	38
McInroy v. Dyer,	61
McKean, Cox v.,	74
McKee v. Gilchrist,	59
McKee's Exr., Comm. v.,	24
McKenzie, Cassiday v.,	22
McKinney v. Snyder,	163
McLallen, Gardner v.,	110
McLaughlin v. Shields,	57
McNeil v. Conwell,	36
McVeagh v. Goods,	22
Mackey, Paull v.,	27, 35
Madden, Thomas v.,	33
Mahon, McClelland v.,	51
Malaun's Admr. v. Ammon,	52
Malone v. Dougherty,	165
Lindsley v.,	52
Man, Drexel v.,	64
Marr, Ins. Co. v.,	38
Mann v. Wieand,	122, 157
Marion Ben. Soc. v. Comm.,	26, 46
Marsh v. Pier,	30
Marshall v. Bobst,	64
Martin, Gicker's Admr. v.,	28
v. Jones,	32
v. McCord,	57
Youst v.,	27
Marvin, Black v.,	59
Mason, Scull v.,	36
Matthews, Mevey v.,	52, 56
May, Snyder v.,	63
Maynard v. Nekervis,	54
Meason v. Kaine,	31, 45
Meeker v. Jackson,	43
Mees, Sweitzer v.,	33
Meighen v. Bank,	57
Menges v. Eyster,	77, 78, 149, 156
Mevey v. Matthews,	52, 56
Michael, Siltzell v.,	42
Mifflin v. Bingham,	62
Miller v. Frazier,	35, 37
v. Garvin's Exr.,	34
Gillespie v.,	27
v. Hayman,	45
Innis v.,	22
v. McClenachan,	32
v. Stem,	38, 59
Milligan, Gallagher v.,	24
Minor v. Neal,	42
Mitchell v. Conrow,	54
Mix v. Smith,	33
Moddewell v. Keever,	52, 56, 160
Molloy, Silliman v.,	42
Mont Alto Iron Co., McFerren v.,	117, 156
Montgomery, Buchanan v.,	59
v. Grant,	24, 58, 59
Moore, Black v.,	43
Moore, David v.,	44
Smith v.,	62
v. Weber,	52, 56
Morehead, McCabe v.,	34
Morris, Davies v.,	46
Morrison v. Hartman,	24, 39
Mortimer, Noble v.,	112
Mott, Harding v.,	54
Muhlenberg's Exrs., Dundas v.,	32
Muirhead v. Kirkpatrick,	53
Mulford v. Downer,	157
Mullen, Byers v.,	27, 59
Murray's Est.,	102
Musser v. Gardner,	94, 96
Mylin's Est.,	72
Myre v. Ludwig,	59
Nav. Co. v. Diffebach,	41
Neal, Minor v.,	42
Neel, Penn. Salt Co. v.,	37
Nekervis, Maynard v.,	54
Nessly v. Swearingen,	38
Newlin v. Newlin,	58
Newman, Dayton v.,	59
Nichols v. Haynes,	163
Noble v. Laley,	52
v. Mortimer,	112
Norman v. Norman,	47, 56
Norris v. Johnston,	51, 58
North v. Turner,	50
Norton, Cox v.,	58
O'Brien v. Davis,	54
O'Brien v. Vantine,	56
O'Connor v. Am. Iron Co.,	76
O'Rourke v. McGrath,	80, 140
Orphans' Court v. Woodburn,	45, 53
Painter, Clover v.,	53
Palmer, Haus v.,	58
Parce v. Stetson,	98
Parke v. Bird,	51
v. Smith,	54
Parker, Swanzey v.,	52, 57, 160, 161
Parkinson, Brown v.,	28
Patterson v. Fay,	64
v. Hagerman,	47
Jones v.,	31
v. Lanning,	83
Lodge v.,	29
Pratt v.,	146, 148, 156
v. Reed,	50, 52
Pattison v. Armstrong,	117, 120
Patton, Ash v.,	42, 50, 64
Paul, Cameron v.,	59
Paull v. Mackey,	27, 35
Peck, Wells v.,	53
Peiffer v. Lytle,	63
Penna. Salt Co. v. Neel,	37
Peres, Enters v.,	27

TABLE OF CASES.

	PAGE
Perot v. Harley,	60
Perry v. Perry,	157, 162
Peters v. Condron,	43
v. Horbach,	52, 56, 64
Willing v.,	50
Phillips, Runkel v.,	111
Phillipy, Kennedy v.,	32
Pier, Marsh v.,	30
Pilling, Scott v.,	54
Pitts. Coal Co. v. Foster,	63
Plank Road Co. v. Ramage,	63
Plumer v. Alexander,	35, 45
Plummer, Fetterman v.,	50
Pollock's Lessee v. Gillespie,	61
Poorman, Carskadden v.,	41
Post v. Avery,	50
Potter v. Burd,	38
Poultney v. Ross,	42
Powers, McFerran v.,	55
Pratt v. Patterson,	146, 148, 156
Prescott v. Borough of Duquesne,	24
Pringle v. Pringle,	92, 94
Prowattain v. Tindall,	158
Purdy, Atkinson v.,	39
Purviance v. Dryden,	32
Pyle v. Pyle,	152
Quinlan v. Davis,	47, 56
Railroad Co. v. Armstrong,	35, 45
Comm. v.,	57
Grayble v.,	25
v. Hickman,	26
v. Johnson,	50, 52
v. Shay,	163
Railway Co. v. Asch,	144
Ralph v. Brown,	40, 47
Ramage, Plank Road Co. v.,	63
Ramsey v. Ramsey,	151
Rance, Salmon v.,	22
Reddig, Gross v.,	94
Reed, Brady v.,	112, 118, 119
Evans's Admr. v.,	144, 146, 148
Humphreys v.,	36, 45
Patterson v.,	50, 52
Rees v. Livingston,	22, 38, 61, 63
Reford, Griffith v.,	54, 63
Rehmer, Dellone v.,	58
Reichenback, Dornick v.,	33
Reid v. Geoghegan,	38
Reigel, Krause v.,	34
Rex v. Bray,	69
Richter v. Cummings,	74
Rick v. Kelly,	54
Riddle, Kidd v.,	42
Ridgely v. Dobson,	47
Ridgway, Seitzinger v.,	27
Riegel v. Wilson,	145
Rhoads v. Armstrong Co.,	24, 25
Bank v.,	89, 90

	PAGE
Rhodes v. Lent,	32
Roberts v. Bye,	34
Robertson v. Stewart,	27
Robinson v. Buck,	61, 64
v. Eldridge,	27, 35
Rodgers, Keyser v.,	43
Rogers, Bingham v.,	44
Rooney v. Campbell,	52
Ross v. Espy,	65
Poultney v.,	42
Roth v. Crissy,	59
Rothrock v. Gallaher,	132, 147, 164
Rowand, McGill v.,	44
Rowland, Updegraff v.,	28
Rowley v. McHugh,	95
Runkel v. Phillips,	111
Rush v. Flickwire,	24, 39
Rutherford's Est.,	106, 131
Ryerss v. Congregation,	24
Rymar, Cleavinger v.,	33
Salmon v. Rance,	22
Sanderson, Douglass v.,	42
Saurman's Exr. v. Bodey,	54
Sawtelle's Appeal,	65
Schalk, Hostetter v.,	122, 125, 126
Schnable v. Koehler,	37
Schnader v. Schnader,	53, 62
School Directors, Barnet v.,	71
Schuylkill Co. v. Copley,	18, 91
Schuylkill Nav. Co. v. Harris,	35, 45, 59
Scott v. Pilling,	54
Scull v. Mason,	36
Search's Appeal,	58
Seip v. Storch,	75, 77, 142
Seitzinger v. Ridgway,	27
Sennett v. Johnston,	64
Seward, Smith v.,	36, 46
Shaffer v. Clark,	158
Shannon v. Comm.,	62
Sharp v. Long,	29
Shaw v. Levy,	42, 47
Shawhan, Jones v.,	32
Shay, Railroad Co. v.,	163
Sheerer v. Lautzerheiser,	35, 45
Sheetz v. Hanbest's Exrs.,	123, 156
Shelly, Walton v.,	53, 54, 69, 89
Shields v. Buchanan,	33, 34
McLaughlin v.,	57
Shinn, Sticker v.,	34
Shippen, Baring v.,	55
Whitney v. (2 W. N. C.), 34, 95, 105, 130, 131, 155	
Whitney v. (8 N.),	34, 106, 131
Shoemaker v. Bank,	57
Shortz v. Unangst,	46
Shultz, Brice v.,	164
Burrows v.,	51
Ins. Co. v.,	121, 156
Siegfried, Christman v.,	37

TABLE OF CASES.

	PAGE
Silliman v. Molloy,	42
Siltzell v. Michael,	42
Simmons, Ins. Co. v.,	59
Simpson, McDowell v.,	45
Simpson's Exr. v. Bovard,	160
Smith, Bickham v.,	64
Bird v.,	33
Boyer v.,	36
Dunlap v.,	62
Karsper v.,	42
Mix v.,	33
v. Moore,	62
Parke v.,	54
v. Seward,	36, 46
v. Thorne,	25, 39
Small v. Jones,	61
Snavely, Doebler v.,	33
Snyder v. Bull,	22
Hatz v.,	53
McKinney v.,	163
v. May,	63
v. Wilt,	54
Wilt v.,	54
v. Wolfley,	43
Solms v. McCulloch,	52, 56, 160
Sommer v. Sommer,	38, 55
Sorg v. First German Cong.,	46
South Creek Twp., Tioga Co. v.,	88, 90
Sower v. Weaver,	93, 157
Soxman, Kerns v.,	58
Spalding, Braine v.,	46
Spence, Clark v.,	44
Spencer, Long v.,	131
Speyerer & Co. v. Bennett's Exrs.,	146
Staley, Crouse v.,	124, 129, 131, 156
Stanbridge v. Catanach,	111
Standley v. Weaver,	41
Stark, Camp v.,	134
Steamboat Dictator v. Heath,	61
Steele v. Ins. Co.,	49, 50, 57, 163
Steininger v. Hoch's Exr.,	58
Steffen v. Hartzell,	37
Stem, Miller v.,	38, 59
Stetson, Parce v.,	98
Sterling v. Trading Co.,	34
Sterrett, Brewster's Adm. v.,	47
Stevenson v. Stevenson,	152
Stewart, Robertson v.,	27
v. Thompson,	60
Sticker v. Shinn,	34
Stille v. Lynch,	54
Stoll v. Weidman,	129
Storch, Scip v.,	75, 77, 142
Strawbridge v. Cartledge,	36
Streper, Buchanan v.,	41, 157
Stroh v. Hess,	34
Stroheckor v. Hoffman,	59
Hoffman v.,	24
Struthers v. Kendall,	45
Stub v. Leis,	36

	PAGE
Summers v. Wallace,	59
Supplee, Gavit v.,	111, 125
Swanzey v. Parker,	52, 57, 160, 161
Swearingen, Nessly v.,	38
Sweitzer's Lessee v. Mees,	33
Tanner, Karns v.,	90, 115, 122, 126, 162
Taylor, Brubaker v.,	139, 164
v. Henderson,	47
Keim v.,	24
v. Kelly,	124, 128, 129
Thomas v. Brady,	63
v. Madden,	33
Thompson v. Bank,	54
Ferree v.,	28, 123
Stewart v.,	60
Thornbury v. Adams Co.,	71
Thorne, Smith v.,	25, 39
Thornton, McGunnagle v.,	45
Tioga Co. v. South Creek Twp.,	88, 90
Tindall, Prowattain v.,	158
Titlow v. Titlow,	29
Tomb, Cambria Iron Co. v.,	52
Trading Co., Sterling v.,	34
Trego v. Huzzard,	63
Trexler, Longswamp v.,	36
Truefitt, Wright v.,	54
Turner, Garsed v.,	64
North v.,	50
Unangst, Shortz v.,	46
Unger v. Wiggins,	37
Union Canal Co. v. Loyd,	42
United States v. Johns,	26
Updegraff v. Rowland,	28
Utt v. Long,	32
Vanartsdalen, Cornell v.,	29, 58
Van Buskirk, Levers v.,	29, 37
Vansant v. Boileau,	23
Vantine, O'Brien v.,	56
Vickers, Wilt v.,	22
Vincent v. Lessee of Huff,	62, 63
Vidal's Appeal,	74, 123, 157
Wagstaff, Cullum v.,	63, 64
Wallace, Bruner v.,	40, 162
Summers v.,	59
Walker, Bank v.,	54
Wistar v.,	50
Waltman v. Herdic,	117, 120
Walton v. Shelly,	53, 54, 69, 89
Wash. Ben. Soc. v. Bacher,	46
Waters, Hinckly v.,	34
Watmough, Comm. v.,	59
Watts v. Leidig,	104, 116, 162
Watson's Est.,	129
Weaver, Sower v.,	93, 157
Standley v.,	41
Yeager v.,	89, 92

TABLE OF CASES.

	PAGE
Weber, Moore v.,	52, 56
Weidman, Stoll v.,	52, 129
Weir, Browne v.,	50
Wells v. Peck,	53
Welsh v. Cooper,	47
Lee v.,	63
West's Admr., McClelland's Exr. v.,	161, 162
Wharton v. Douglass,	64
Wheeler's Est.,	148
Whipper's Est.,	157
Whitaker, Yerkes v.,	143, 144
White, Ballentine v.,	92, 158
Whitehead v. Bank,	56
White's Estate,	42
Whitesell v. Crane,	44
Whitney, Agnew v.,	106
v. Shippen (2 W. N. C.),	34, 95, 105, 130, 131, 155
v. Shippen (8 N.),	34, 106, 131
Wickham, Willard v.,	59
Wieand, Mann v.,	122, 157
Wiggins, Unger v.,	37
Wightman, Lothrop v.,	27, 64
Wikoff, Bank v.,	61
Wilbur, Derrickson v.,	97
Willard v. Wickham,	59
Williams, Bennett v.,	76
v. Davis,	159, 163
McIldowney v.,	55
Willing v. Peters,	50
Wilson, Cawley v.,	92, 131
v. Clarion Co.,	71
Riegel v.,	147
Wilt v. Snyder,	54
Snyder v.,	54
v. Vickers,	22
Winter v. Winter,	152
Wise v. Dispensary,	144
Wistar v. Walker,	50
Wolf v. Batchelder,	76
v. Carothers,	40
v. Finks,	51
Wolfinger v. Forsman,	22
Wolfley, Snyder v.,	43
Wood, Bank v.,	40
Woodburn, Orphans' Court v.,	45, 53
Woods, Hartz v.,	31
Work v. Kase,	54
v. McClay,	40
Wray, Hanna v.,	110, 154
Wright v. Funk,	162
Lincoln v.,	28
v. Truefitt,	54
Yeager v. Weaver,	89, 92
Yerkes v. Whitaker,	143, 144
Yonng's Estate,	102
Young's Exrs., Anderson v.,	63
Youst v. Martin,	27
Zeigler v. Gray,	38

PART I.

THE COMMON LAW OF THE STATE RELATING TO THE INCOMPETENCY OF WITNESSES.

CHAPTER I.

THE INCOMPETENCY OF WITNESSES.

The incompetency of witnesses will be first considered as it existed and still exists under certain circumstances in this State, unaffected by legislation. Up to this time legislation has so cautiously undertaken the removal of disabilities as to still leave the common law of the State in many cases absolutely untouched. In order, therefore, to apply the recent legislation to the cases which now arise, it is essential that not only the new laws should be known, but the old law also, as it existed prior to any of the enabling acts. It is proposed, therefore, to give a short sketch of the common law relating to the incompetency of witnesses in this State, particularly that relating to interest, without reference to any statutes, and to follow this by an historical résumé of the acts, with such rules for their practical application as may suggest themselves.

Incompetency of Witnesses.—Evidence in courts of justice is that obtained from competent witnesses under the sanction of a legal oath, *i. e.*, an oath as ordinarily understood, or its legal equivalent. Persons offered as witnesses may be either competent or incompetent; in the latter case they are not permitted to testify. At common law the incompetency of persons called as witnesses is either (1) *General*, or (2) *Special*.

General Incompetency is such as renders the witness incompetent to testify at any time and in any case so long as the disqualifying circumstances exist.

Special Incompetency only disqualifies a witness otherwise competent from testifying in a particular case, because of the relation which he bears to it or persons interested in it.

Incompetent Testimony is such testimony as, without regard to the competency or incompetency of the witness giving it, the court declines to hear, as (*a*) confidential communications of husband and wife, (*b*) confidential communications of counsel and client, (*c*) communications between state officials, and (*d*) certain facts regarded as indecent or improper and not to be mentioned.

Incompetent Witnesses.—It is neither necessary nor desirable to consider the subject of incompetent testimony, since no legislation has in any manner changed that, but it is important to have pointed out and to observe the difference between the incompetency of testimony and that of witnesses.

General Incompetency.—General incompetency arises either from the actual or professed inability to feel the sanctity of an oath, as in the case of (*a*) idiots and lunatics, (*b*) intoxicated persons, (*c*) children too young to understand the sanctity of an oath, and (*d*) persons who do not believe in the existence of God or a future state of punishment for perjury; or from the presumption of law that an oath when taken will be disregarded, as (*e*) in the case of a person convicted of an infamous crime.

It is aside from our purpose to treat of those cases of general incompetency which rest upon actual or professed inability to feel the sanctity of an oath. We will discuss only those cases of incompetency, whether general or special, which have been affected by legislation. There is but one case of general incompetency resulting from the presumption of law that an oath when taken will be disregarded, that of persons convicted of infamous crimes. "Infamous crimes are treason, felony, and every species of the *crimen falsi*, such as forgery, perjury, subornation of perjury, and offences affecting the public administration of justice, such as bribing a witness to absent himself, and not to give evidence, and conspiracies to obstruct the administration of justice, or falsely to accuse one of an indictable crime. 2 Russell on Crimes, 973; 1 Greenleaf's Ev., § 373. This is clearly the limitation of infamous crimes as understood in this State."[1] The disability resulting from

---

[1] Per AGNEW, J., Schuylkill Co. *v.* Copley, 17 Sm., 386; Starkey on Evidence, p. *118, note 1, 9th Am. ed.

conviction of an infamous crime was always removed by a pardon for the offence; and by the Act of March 31st, 1860,[1] the serving out a sentence of imprisonment at labor was rendered equivalent to a pardon, except in the case of wilful and corrupt perjury.

Special Incompetency.—This arises wholly from the presumption of law that an oath when taken will not be regarded, or from the policy of the law as conducive to good morals and the peace of society. To the former reason are referred the cases of (*a*) parties, (*b*) interested persons, out of which also grew the incompetency of parties to negotiable paper to impeach it, and that of the assignor of a chose in action to sustain it; and to both reasons is ascribed the case of (*c*) husband and wife testifying for or against each' other.

With the exception of the case of husband and wife, all of the cases of special incompetency were really, as will be seen, the outgrowth of the disability arising from interest, and this, so far as it excluded husband and wife from testifying in favor of each other, arose from the same cause. The disability of husband and wife to testify against each other arose rather from the policy of the law, which deemed it to be for the best interests of society and conducive to domestic happiness that in this relation neither party should have the opportunity of appearing against the other's interest in any way. But in either case whichever way the testimony might tend the rule was simple and absolute, that wherever the interest of one existed the other was incompetent. To understand when either is to be excluded, therefore, we must understand the general subject of exclusion on the ground of interest. We will then consider at some length the subject of incompetency arising from interest, since from it we can test that arising from the relation of husband and wife, and also see the development of the other grounds of exclusion said to be the outgrowth of this.

---

[1] Purdon's Dig., 371, pl. 301.

CHAPTER II.

INCOMPETENCY ARISING FROM INTEREST.

Interested Persons.—Although, as will be seen hereafter, the rule excluding the testimony of parties in this State was eventually made to rest upon public policy, based upon quite different reasons from that of interest in the suit, it unquestionably had its origin in the common law, in the presumption of the want of integrity of those interested in the event of the cause, than whom in most cases none could be more interested than the parties themselves. It will, therefore, be more convenient to consider the ultimate outgrowth of this theory in its natural order as an historical development.

Interest has always been recognized as a good ground for the exclusion of a witness, whether he be an actual party or merely one interested in the event of the suit.

Gilbert says:[1] "Those who are totally excluded from all testimony for want of integrity are:

"*First.* Persons interested in the matter in question; and here the general rule is, that no man can be a witness for himself, but he is the best witness that can be against himself. See 2 Atk. Rep., 615." . . . (And after considering the subject of interest, he proceeds, p. 130): "From the first rule several other corollaries may be deduced.

"1st, That the plaintiff or defendant cannot be a witness in his own cause, for these are the persons that have a most immediate interest, and it is not to be presumed that a man who complains without cause, or defends without justice, should have honesty enough to confess it." Peake says:[2] "Section III. *Of persons incompe-*

---

[1] Gilbert on Evidence, p. 120.   [2] Peake's Evidence, p. *144.

tent by reason of their interest in the cause. But the rule which has the most extensive operation in the exclusion of witnesses, and which has been found most difficult in its application, is that which prevents persons interested in the event of a suit (unless in a few excepted cases of evident necessity) from being witnesses in it." . . After discussing the nature of interest: "From what has been already said, it may be taken as a general rule that a party in a cause cannot be examined as a witness, for he is in the highest degree interested in the event of it, and though he be barely trustee for another, he has still an interest sufficient to render him incompetent, for he is personally answerable in the first instance for the costs of the suit, and the *chance* he may have of indemnity from the person for whom he acts does not remove the interest which the *certain* liability creates in him. But where a man is not in point of fact at all interested, he may be examined."

It remains to determine what interest is. *Interest, as a ground for the exclusion of the testimony of a proffered witness, must be a legal, certain, and immediate pecuniary interest in the result of the issue, or in the record as an instrument of evidence.*

It must be a *pecuniary* interest. With the single exception of the relation of husband and wife, no relation, however close or powerful in its influence, is sufficient to exclude, unless it involve a pecuniary interest; as was said by GIBSON, C. J., in Bennett *v.* Hethington, 16 S. & R., 195: "Although the case of the witness be, in every point and particular, the case of the party by whom he is called to testify; although he expects a benefit from the event; and, in short, although he be subject to as strong a *bias* as can influence the understanding and actions of man; *yet, if he be not implicated in the legal consequences of the judgment, he is competent.*"

It must be *legal*. No mere honorary obligation on the part of the witness to make good a possible loss to be occasioned by the suit, nor the hope or expectation that the party for whom he is called will so far regard an honorary obligation as to benefit the witness if successful, nor indeed the most well-founded expectation that the witness will derive benefit or injury from the result of the suit, will exclude, unless the expectation is founded upon a legal relation between the parties capable of being enforced by law.[1] It is true that some of the earlier cases in this State held a contrary view, but they were soon, if not in terms, yet practically, overruled.[2]

It must be *certain*. When the very question at issue involves the question whether the witness is interested or not, the court ought not to assume that he is, and so exclude him. As in an action on a joint and several bond against the legal representatives of one of the obligors, under a plea of *non est factum*, the obligor not joined in the suit was competent (not being otherwise interested) at the call of the defendant, because to exclude him would be to assume the very point at issue before it was tried.[3]

It must be *immediate*. The interest must be one existing at the time the evidence is offered; not that which may have existed at one time, but has ceased to exist before the witness is called (except so far as public policy in certain cases qualifies this rule. See p. 52). As where the statute of limitations has intervened to bar a responsibility imposed upon the witness,[4] or he has parted with property which so long as he was owner or holder of it was accompanied by certain obligations from which he has thus been exonerated.[5] And when the testimony of a witness has been taken at a time when he was disinterested and he has subsequently acquired an interest, his deposition, taken at the time when he was competent, is admissible.[6]

---

[1] 1 Greenleaf on Evidence, § 388; Long *v.* Bailie, 4 S. & R., 222; Wilt *v.* Vickers, 8 W., 227; Rees *v.* Livingston, 5 Wr., 113; Cassiday *v.* McKenzie, 4 W. & S., 282.

[2] See McVeaugh *v.* Goods, 1 Dall., 62; Innis *v.* Miller, 2 Dall., 50.

[3] Ely *v.* Hager, 3 B., 154, and see Snyder *v.* Bull, 5 H., 54.

[4] Ludlow *v.* Insurance Company, 2 S. & R., 119. Salmon *v.* Rance, 3 S. & R., 311.

[5] Irvine *v.* The Bank, 2 W. & S., 190.

[6] Wolfinger *v.* Forsman, 6 B., 294.

Finally, the interest must be one in the result of the issue or in the record as an instrument of evidence. It would be a useless undertaking to cite all of the cases in which the existence or non-existence of interest has been judicially ascertained. Until within the past ten or fifteen years, probably no subject was a more fruitful theme for discussion than that of the competency of witnesses, viewed not only with reference to the interest originally existing, but also with reference to the means of removing it. Most of the cases of interest originally existing, however, can be pretty fairly resolved into a few general classes.

Interest in the Result of the Issue.—It will be found that a witness's interest in the result of the issue will affect either,

    a. His liability for costs, or,

    b. A fund in which he will be legally entitled to share, and which will be created, enlarged, or diminished by the result of the suit.

(*a.*) *The Liability for Costs.*—This will, of course, arise: (1.) Where the witness called is a party in his own right, either as plaintiff or defendant, and though he might relieve himself from all interest whatever in the result of the suit, the liability for costs would be sufficient, even without other reasons, to render him incompetent. (2.) Where a party to the cause has no beneficial interest whatever in the suit, but is personally liable for the costs, this is a good ground for his exclusion, as in the case of an executor under an alleged will, plaintiff in a feigned issue to test the validity of the paper offered, he is liable for costs and incompetent. There was just this difference at common law between parties and persons not parties, that in the first case the presumption always was that they were incompetent; in the other, the presumption was that they were competent.[1]

It is not, however, every one whose name appears upon the record who is liable directly for costs. The contractor in a *sci. fa.*

---

[1] Vansant *v.* Boileau, 1 Binn., 444.

sur mechanic's lien is not liable to the plaintiff for costs,[1] nor a mere trustee, formally a party to the record in the right of his *cestui que trust*.[2] So, too, where a party's name has been put upon the record erroneously.[3] (3.) On the other hand, it frequently happens that the liability for costs rests upon one who is not named upon the record at all, and in that event he is quite as incompetent by reason of this liability as though he were actually a party. This occurs whenever the witness was beneficially interested at the commencement of the suit as plaintiff; as where, under contract with the nominal plaintiff, he is to receive a portion of the fund recovered;[4] or where he is, under a similar arrangement, beneficially interested as defendant.[5] The rule also applies in the case of persons beneficially interested in a feigned issue.[6]

(4.) And lastly, in the case of one not a party to the record, whose interest in the recovery of plaintiff and defendant is evenly balanced, but in one event he will be liable over to one or the other for the costs of the suit. This will determine his incompetency; as when replevin has been brought by one whose goods have been levied on for the rent of another, the tenant would be liable over to the plaintiff not only for the value of the goods but for the costs also, in the event of a failure to recover in this suit, and would, therefore, be incompetent for him;[7] or, in suit against the security on a bond, the principal debtor would be liable over to the defendant for the costs of that suit in case of the recovery of a judgment against him, and he is therefore incompetent;[8] and this is true of any other case in which it would be legally possible for

---

[1] Dickinson College *v.* Church, 1 W. & S., 462.
[2] Ryerss *v.* Congregation of Blossburg, 9 C., 114; Keim *v.* Taylor, 1 J., 163.
[3] Prescott *v.* Borough of Duquesne, 12 Wr., 118.
[4] Gallagher *v.* Milligan, 3 P. & W., 177; Rhoads *v.* Armstrong Co., 5 Wr., 92.
[5] Hoffman *v.* Strohecker, 9 W., 183.
[6] Montgomery *v.* Grant, 7 Sm., 243.
[7] Rush *v.* Flickwir, 17 S. & R., 82.
[8] Morrison *v.* Hartman, 2 H., 55; Comm. *v.* McKee's Ex., 2 Gr., 27.

the costs of the suit to be added to a debt already due.[1] In such a case this circumstance will turn the scale.

(*b.*) *Interest in a Fund.*—The result of the suit may affect a fund in which the witness will be legally entitled to share, in the case of:

(1.) Inhabitants of a borough, township, or city.
(2.) Members of a private corporation, or unincorporated society, and partners.
(3.) Debtors or creditors of one of the parties.
(4.) Assignors entitled to a surplus of the land or property assigned.
(5.) Heirs and legatees.

(1.) *Inhabitants.*—No more striking instance of the possible disadvantages of an irrefragable rule, which however reasonable in its origin, becomes absurd when pushed to its purely logical conclusion, could be cited than that which rendered the inhabitant of a district in which he was assessed for taxation incompetent to testify on behalf of the corporation in a suit to recover a penalty. In the English common law it would seem that the public disadvantage attending the strict enforcement of the rule made an exception in favor of competency, if no purely personal interest intervened;[2] but, in the opinion of DUNCAN, J., the exception did not exist in this State, although the benefit of it was secured in the case before him by a most delicate refinement between *rated* and *ratable* inhabitants, the former of whom "the court could entertain no doubt, that such immediate, direct, and certain interest would exclude;" but since the latter "might never be rated; he might cease to be an inhabitant, or become exempt from taxation," he was held competent.[3] The disadvantageous working of the rule of exclusion seems to have become apparent in this class of cases first, and as we shall see, the remedy of legislation was very early applied to it.

---

[1] Smith *v.* Thorne, 9 W., 144; Davenport *v.* Freeman, 3 W. & S., 557; Rhoads *v.* Armstrong Co., 5 Wr., 92.

[2] Greenleaf on Evidence, § 331.   [3] Comm. *v.* Baird, 4 S. & R., 141.

(2.) *Members of a Private Corporation or Society and Partners.*—Nearly analogous to the case of the inhabitants of a district is that of the members of a corporation, who are of course on the one hand interested in increasing the funds of the corporation, to a certain share of which they are entitled, and on the other in saving its funds from depletion by a recovery against it. Thus, in a suit by a railroad company to recover a subscription to stock,[1] or in a suit against the directors of a corporation under an act to recover the amount of a corporation debt, which if successful would exonerate the company,[2] the stockholders are incompetent witnesses for the company in the one case or the plaintiff in the other. And when an insurance company would be exonerated from the payment of a policy if the prosecution of the owner for destroying his vessel should be successful, the president of the company, who was also a stockholder, was incompetent for the prosecution,[3] but the mere fact of being an officer is not a ground for exclusion if the witness is not a party to the suit nor a stockholder.[4] Where one has been a stockholder and surrendered his shares, or sold them, he is competent for the corporation in a suit to recover a claim if the corporation is solvent and no personal liability thereby attaches;[5] but if the surrender or sale of shares to the corporation has been upon a guarantee that they shall bring a certain price, the direct legal interest of the witness in keeping up the value of the stock in general by saving the capital from depletion is sufficient to render him incompetent.[6]

In the case of unincorporated societies the same rule applies when the result of the suit would be to diminish a fund in which the members are entitled to share in case of a recovery against the society.[7]

---

[1] Phila. & W. C. RR. Co. v. Hickman, 4 C., 318.
[2] Hill v. Frazier, 10 Ii., 320.   [3] U. S. v. Johns, 4 Dall., 412.
[4] Phila. Ins. Co. v. Wash. Ins. Co., 11 H., 250.
[5] Bank v. Green, 3 W., 374; Irvine v. Lumbermen's Bank, 2 W. & S., 190.
[6] Grayble v. York and Getts. RR. Co., 10 S. & R., 269.
[7] The Marion Ben. Soc. v. Cowan, 7 C., 82, S. C., 2 Ph., 129.

(3.) *Creditors.*—In ordinary cases the interest which a creditor has in the recovery or loss of his debtor is too remote and contingent to affect his competency in a suit to which the debtor is a party. The mere possible increase of the funds of a debtor will not preclude his creditor from testifying in his favor in a suit brought by him.[1] Nor will the possible decrease of his property, and consequent greater inability to pay his debts, render his creditor incompetent for him when he is defendant.[2] So in a suit in which an estate is a party, when it does not appear that the estate is insolvent a creditor may be a witness for it.[3] A doubt was expressed in Byers *v.* Mullen, 9 W., 266, whether the creditor of an insolvent estate was competent, and in Seitzinger *v.* Ridgway, 4 W. & S., 472, where a witness called by the plaintiff in a suit in partition to establish title declared that he held a judgment against him, and that there was a "slim chance" of getting his money unless the plaintiff was successful, he was held incompetent. On general principles it would seem that while insolvency on the part of the debtor himself ought not to render the creditor incompetent, because the chance of his being deprived of any portion of his claim is purely contingent and rests only upon the assumption that the debtor will remain insolvent forever, yet where the debtor is dead, so that the amount of his estate out of which the debt is to be paid is actually fixed, and the result of the suit must therefore materially affect its amount, in such case if the estate is shown to be insolvent the creditor would be incompetent; this distinction, however, does not seem to have been raised by any case in this State. But where by any contract with the debtor the payment of a creditor's debt is made dependent upon the debtor's success in the suit, the creditor is incompetent.[4] As the relation of debtor and creditor does not neces-

[1] Robertson *v.* Stewart, 5 W., 442; Gillespie *v.* Miller, 1 Wr., 247.

[2] Enters *v.* Peres, 2 R., 279; McCaskey *v.* Graff, 11 H., 321; Lothrop *v.* Wightman, 5 Wr., 297.

[3] Youst *v.* Martin, 3 S. & R., 427; Boyer *v.* Kendall, 14 S. & R., 178; Jones *v.* Brownfield, 2 B., 55; 1 Greenleaf on Evidence, § 389.

[4] Robinson *v.* Eldridge, 10 S. & R., 140; Paull *v.* Mackey, 3 W., 110.

sarily preclude the creditor from testifying at the call of the debtor when defendant, still less does it do so when called by the plaintiff, as where, in a suit to charge one as owner of a ship for supplies, other creditors in a like situation with the plaintiff are competent at his call to prove the assumption of liability by the defendant,[1] for this is a mere interest in the question, which, while of practical value to the witness, is not a legal interest in this particular suit. It sometimes has happened that the question of the competency of a creditor has arisen in a contest between two other creditors, or a creditor and purchaser from his debtor, over a fund or property to which both lay claim, but in which the witness has no rights; in this case it is clear that there is no interest of the witness in this fund to be affected by the result of the suit, and he is therefore competent,[2] as in a feigned issue between a judgment creditor and a purchaser at sheriff's sale under another judgment to test the validity of the first, a third creditor is incompetent. In contests between creditors over a fund or property to which both lay claim, the interest of the debtor has already been extinguished by the lien acquired by both of the claimants, one of which, it is true as between themselves, may have a priority over the other, but both of which, so far as this record would be evidence, are sufficient as against the debtor; as in the cases cited above[3] of a contest between the assignee of a claim from a debtor and a creditor who has seized the assigned claim in attachment execution, or where a bill in equity is filed by one creditor to compel the transfer to him of stock alleged to have been mistakenly transferred to another creditor, the debtor, having lost his interest in the stock is competent.[4]

(4.) *Assignors Entitled to a Surplus of the Fund or Property Assigned.*—When an assignment of the fund or property in dispute

[1] Lincoln *v.* Wright, 11 H., 76.

[2] Gicker's Admr. *v.* Martin, 14 Wr., 138; Updegraff *v.* Rowland, 2 Sm., 317; Brown *v.* Parkinson, 6 Sm., 336.

[3] Updegraff *v.* Rowland, 2 Sm., 317, and Ferree *v.* Thompson, 2 Sm., 353.

[4] Finney's Appeal, 9 Sm., 398.

has been made, but the assignor retains an interest in the same after payment of certain claims out of it, he is incompetent at the call of the assignee, who seeks either to secure or increase it, or where an assignment has been made for the benefit of creditors, whether the assignor has an interest in the surplus or not, for he has at any rate an interest in having his debts paid out of the assigned estate.[1]

(5.) *Heirs and Legatees.*—The interest of an heir or distributee under the statute in the estate of his ancestor or intestate, and the interest of one entitled under a will to a distributive share of the estate is such as to exclude under any circumstances, because the distributive share to be received by the heir or distributee must be affected by the suit.[2] But where there is a legatee of a specific sum or thing, unless there is proof of the insolvency of the estate (in which case the amount of the estate would materially affect the amount of the legacy), it is a matter of indifference to the legatee whether the estate gains or loses its suit, and he is therefore competent.[3] Where the question of the validity of an alleged will has been made the subject of a feigned issue, a legatee under a previous will is competent to testify against the will, the validity of which is on trial, because the verdict in this case would not establish the validity of the will under which he claims.[4]

Interest in the Record as an Instrument of Evidence.—The record of a judgment rendered in a previous suit may be evidence of the very fact in issue, or of a collateral fact necessary to obtaining a verdict. The record of a final judgment is conclusive evidence of the facts directly put in issue by it as against parties or privies in a subsequent suit upon the same issue between

---

[1] Sharp *v.* Long, 4 C., 433; Carey *v.* Bright, 8 Sm., 70.

[2] Kimball *v.* Kimball, 3 R., 469; Lodge *v.* Patterson, 3 W., 74; Dimond *v.* McDowell, 7 W., 510; Buchanan *v.* Buchanan, 10 Wr., 186.

[3] Levers *v.* Van Buskirk, 4 B., 309; Cornell *v.* Vanartsdalen, Id., 364.

[4] Titlow *v.* Titlow, 4 Sm., 216.

the same parties or those claiming under them, in which case also it may be pleaded in bar of the actions;[1] as where, "if P. brings an action for the price of goods against N., the record of the judgment is admissible and conclusive on the issue of property in replevin for the same goods, brought by P. against a purchaser under N.; and this whether the judgment be for the plaintiff or the defendant in the first action,"[2] or the judgment in an action of ejectment, which binds all the parties and all persons claiming under them.

As against strangers to a cause the record of the judgment is not conclusive evidence nor pleadable in bar of the action, and yet it may be evidence for or against them of certain collateral facts necessary to be proven in order to obtain a final judgment, as "to prove the amount which a principal has been compelled to pay for the default of his agent; or the amount which a surety has been compelled to pay for the principal debtor; and, in general, to show the fact, that the judgment was actually rendered at such a time and for such an amount."[3] For this reason a person who is no party to a proceeding may yet be interested in the judgment, since the record of it may be used as an instrument of evidence for or against him in a subsequent suit, which is usually the result of such judgment. Interest in the record as an instrument of evidence exists when the record may be used,

(*a.*) *To Shift the Burden of All or Part of a Debt from the Witness.*—When one is *prima facie* liable to pay a debt, but suit is brought against another, the original debtor is incompetent to prove anything by which it would appear that the defendant was liable for all or part of the debt, so that in the event of a recovery by the plaintiff the record would be evidence on which to base a subsequent suit against the witness by showing that the debt had been

---

[1] 1 Greenleaf on Evid., §§ 523–531.
[2] Marsh *v.* Pier, 4 R., 273.
[3] 1 Greenleaf on Evid., § 527; Starkie on Evid., p. 323 *et seq.*

already paid; or in a subsequent suit by the witness to exact contributions from a co-obligor. Where one has been dealing as principal, in a suit against a third party as principal, he is incompetent at the call of the plaintiff to prove that he was only an agent, and so shift the burden of the debt upon the defendant;[1] so in a suit against a director under the corporation act to recover the amount of a corporation debt, where in case of judgment the corporation would be exonerated, the stockholders are incompetent;[2] or in a suit on a promise to pay the debt of another in consideration of an assignment of security to the defendant by the original debtor, he is incompetent at the call of the plaintiff to prove the promise of the defendant and the fulfilment of the condition by himself;[3] but the same objection would not apply upon a mere unconditional promise to pay, for the recovery of the plaintiff in that case would not shift the burden of the debt from the debtor, but merely change the direction of its payment, and the judgment, so far from being an instrument of evidence for the witness in a subsequent suit against him by the promisor, would be evidence against him.[4] In ejectment by a vendor of land against a purchaser at sheriff's sale from the vendee, who had given his promissory note for a portion of the balance of the purchase-money, the vendee is incompetent at the call of the plaintiff to prove notice to the defendant of the amount due, and that the balance was still unpaid.[5] A similar case arises in suit by *sci. fa. sur* mortgage against property purchased at sheriff's sale subject to the mortgage, where the issue is payment or discharge; the mortgagor is incompetent for the plaintiff, because his recovery would shift the payment of the loan from himself to the purchaser, who would have no recovery over.[6] So, too, the purchaser of a house subject to a mechanic's

---

[1] Hickling v. Fitch, 1 M., 208; Meason v. Kaine, 13 Sm., 335.
[2] Hill v. Frazier, 10 H., 320.
[3] Hayes v. Gudykunst, 1 J., 221.
[4] Ibid.
[5] Long v. Long, 1 W., 265; Jones v. Patterson, 1 W. & S., 321.
[6] Hartz v. Woods, 8 B., 471; Hansell v. Lutz, 8 H., 284.

lien is incompetent for the defendant in suit on a *sci. fa.* to prove that the lien was improperly filed;[1] and in a suit against the estate of a lunatic to recover witness fees incurred by the committee of the lunatic, for which, of course, the committee is primarily responsible, the committee is incompetent for the plaintiff to shift the burden of payment upon the estate.[2] Of course the rule which applies to shifting the burden of all of a debt applies to any part of it, and it is equally incompetent for the debtor to show a joint responsibility with him.[3] In suits against alleged partners, one of them is incompetent at the call of the plaintiff to prove the partnership, or to prove that a payment to himself was on the firm account,[4] or any other fact tending to exonerate him from part of the debt,[5] or giving him the right to obtain contribution from his co-obligor,[6] while he is equally incompetent in a suit against his co-obligor to testify in his behalf, because that would be to exonerate him from his liability to contribution (in the event of a judgment against the defendant).[7] When the right to contribution does not arise, however, as in a suit against one of two joint trespassers, the other is not incompetent for him,[8] nor is he incompetent for the plaintiff.[9]

It may happen that the suit is against one whom it is alleged has become jointly or solely responsible for the claim originally good against the witness, which allegation, if proven, would exonerate the witness, and enable him to use the record as a bar to a subsequent action against himself. As in a suit for a legacy against one

---

[1] Jones *v.* Shawhan, 4 W. & S., 257; and see also Leib *v.* Childs, 3 Cl., 70 (D. C.).

[2] Utt *v.* Long, 6 W. & S., 174.

[3] Rhodes *v.* Lent, 3 W., 364.

[4] Miller *v.* McClenachan, 1 Y., 144; Purviance *v.* Dryden, 3 S. & R., 402.

[5] Heckert *v.* Fegley, 6 W. & S., 139.

[6] Henderson *v.* Lewis, 9 S. & R., 379.

[7] Martin *v.* Jones, 6 B., 82.

[8] Entriken *v.* Brown, 8 C., 364.

[9] Kennedy *v.* Phillipy, 1 H., 408; Dundas *v.* Muhlenberg's Exrs., 11 C., 351.

of two executors, who is alleged to have received the fund, his coexecutor is incompetent on behalf of the plaintiff to prove that fact,[1] and one who is alleged to have paid an agent a debt due to his principal is incompetent to prove it[2] in a suit by the principal against the agent.

(*b.*) *To Exonerate from a Secondary Liability.*—Wherever property, either real or personal, has been parted with, and at the time of the assignment there is given an actual or implied warranty or guarantee by the vendor or assignor, he is incompetent in a suit brought either by or against his vendee or assignee, the record of which might be used as evidence of the measure of damages in a claim against him on his warranty or guarantee. Thus in the case of land, a vendor with general warranty, or with an implied warranty of title, is incompetent to sustain the title of his vendee in ejectment brought by or against the vendee.[3] But where the vendor has conveyed without any warranty at all,[4] or has given only a special warranty, and no other is implied, he is competent.[5] The vendor may testify in either case against his title,[6] and in ejectment by his vendee he may prove the sale and payment of the purchase-money.[7] So where the vendor has conveyed with a general warranty as to title only, he is competent for his vendee in a suit for damages against him for disturbance of a right of way,[8] and when he has conveyed without a covenant against a known defect, he is competent for the vendee in an action by him to recover damages

---

[1] Doebler *v.* Snavely, 5 W., 225.   [2] Hayes *v.* Grier, 4 Binn., 80.

[3] Shields *v.* Buchanan, 2 Y., 219; Patterson *v.* Lanning, 10 W., 135; Goodman *v.* Losey, 3 W. & S., 526.

[4] Dornick *v.* Reichenback, 10 S. & R., 84; Bird *v.* Smith, 8 W., 434; Thomas *v.* Madden, 14 Wr., 261.

[5] Lessee of Sweitzer *v.* Mees, 6 Binn., 500; Beidelman *v.* Foulk, 5 W., 308; Cleavinger *v.* Rymar, 3 W. & S., 486.

[6] Brown *v.* Downing, 4 S. & R., 494.

[7] Mix *v.* Smith, 7 B., 75.

[8] Greenwalt *v.* Horner, 6 S. & R., 71.

therefor,[1] and for the plaintiff in an action against his vendee, who took subject to a charge sought to be enforced.[2] Where the vendor has conveyed merely as trustee he is competent,[3] because in this, as in all of the exceptions noted, the issue is not upon a point which would render the record an instrument of evidence, either for or against the witness, in any subsequent suit against him upon his warranty. In the case of the vendor of personal property there is an implied warranty of title, and the vendor is incompetent in a contest between two of his alleged vendees,[4] because of his liability over for costs.

In the case of the assignor of a chose in action, it is true that his incompetency to sustain it was determined by reason of the policy of law, apart from the existence of interest; but that would be sufficient of itself, unless removed, to render him incompetent, there being always, if not a special guarantee, at least an implied warranty that the claim is due; in either case, therefore, he would be incompetent to sustain that issue,[5] and it is immaterial whether the claim is actually itself sued upon, or is only used as a set-off by the defendant.[6] On the other hand, if the issue be payment of the claim subsequent to the time when the assignment was made, he is equally incompetent for the defendant in a suit by the assignee, because a verdict for defendant would likewise exonerate him.[7]

In the case of sureties on bonds and recognizances, where judgment for the principal would exonerate the surety, as bail for the

---

[1] Krause v. Reigel, 2 Wh., 386.   [2] Roberts v. Bye, 6 C., 375.

[3] Lessee of Shields v. Buchanan, 2 Y., 219.

[4] McCabe v. Morehead, 1 W. & S., 513; Whitney v. Shippen, 2 W. N. C., 470; Whitney v. Shippen, 8 N., 22.

[5] Kelly v. Eichman, 5 Wh., 446; Sticker v. Shinn, 5 Wh., 452; McGinn v. Holmes, 2 W., 121; Stroh v. Hess, 1 W. & S., 147.

[6] Hinckley v. Waters, 9 W., 179.

[7] Sterling v. Trading Co., 11 S. & R., 179; Miller v. Garvin's Exr., 12 S. & R., 100.

defendant in an action for erecting a nuisance, or the surety on a replevin bond, the surety is incompetent.[1]

(c.) *Where the Record may be Used by the Witness to Sustain a Claim.*—Where a conditional contract exists between the witness and one of the parties to the suit, the condition of which is the success or failure in the suit, the record would be evidence to enforce that contract, or as a defence in its enforcement, and such a witness is therefore incompetent.[2]

(d.) *To Fix Liability upon Him when not prima facie Responsible.*—This sort of interest is that which affects the testimony of agents, or others, against whom the record may be used as evidence to fix liabilities upon them, in a suit to recover back a loss to which they have contributed. It exists in the case of an agent when his principal or employer is sued for the negligence of the agent. The record is "not evidence to establish his (the agent's) liability, but admissible to show the *quantum* of damages. His liability must be shown by other proof."—STRONG, J.[3] As will be seen hereafter, an agent is ordinarily a competent witness for his principal (p. 44); but he is incompetent, when the question at issue is the negligence or fraud of the agent or servant, and a judgment against the principal would entitle him to recoup himself in a suit against the agent, either for damages recovered against him where he was defendant;[4] or for damages or charges which he failed to recover in a suit brought by himself, because of the negligence of his servant; as in a suit by the owner of a canal-boat to recover damages for a collision, where the contributory negligence of plaintiff's captain or pilot prevented a recovery;[5] or where injury to

---

[1] Miller *v.* Frazier, 3 W., 456; Dannels *v.* Fitch, 8 B., 495.

[2] Robinson *v.* Eldridge, 10 S. & R., 140; Paull *v.* Mackey, 3 W., 110.

[3] Dodge *v.* Bacher, 2 Pitts., 487.

[4] Sheerer *v.* Lautzerheiser, 6 W., 551; Dorrance *v.* Comm., 1 H., 160; Loudon Sav. F. Soc. *v.* Hagerstown Sav. Bank, 12 C., 498; Catawissa RR. Co. *v.* Armstrong, 13 Wr., 186.

[5] Schuyl. C. Nav. Co. *v.* Harris, 5 W. & S., 28; Plumer *v.* Alexander, 2 J., 81.

goods intrusted to a common carrier resulting from the negligence of his servant was taken as a defence to an action for freight;[1] but the rule does not extend to the employee of an agent.[2] In order to exclude the agent under these circumstances, however, it is necessary that the agency of the proffered witness in the very transaction in question should be shown, and that the question at issue is his negligence.[3] Not unlike this case, too, is that of an executor in a suit against the estate under pleas admitting assets, where the record, in case of recovery, would be evidence to charge the executor personally in case of his squandering the funds,[4] or that of the contractor, who has been fully paid, in *sci. fa. sur* mechanic's lien, who is incompetent to testify for the defendant.[5] Where the result of a recovery by one against whom a witness is called would be to show that the witness had unlawfully incurred a liability, to enforce which the record would be evidence against him, he is incompetent. For example, where one has been in possession of land after ejectment was brought, holding under the same title as the defendant, he is an incompetent witness on his behalf, because of his liability over to the plaintiff, if he is successful, for mesne profits;[6] so where one has acted as executor under a will, he is incompetent to sustain it;[7] and one acting in a fiduciary capacity, who has paid money without authority upon a promise to repay, is incompetent for the plaintiff in a suit by his principal to enforce the promise.[8] And the liability may have

---

[1] Humphreys v. Reed, 6 Wh., 435.

[2] Comm. v. Allen, 6 C., 49.

[3] Smith v. Seward, 3 B., 342; Scull v. Mason, 7 Wr., 99; Dodge v. Bache, 2 Pitts., 487.

[4] Conrad v. Keyser, 5 S. & R., 370.

[5] Dickinson Coll. v. Church, 1 W. & S., 462.

[6] Strawbridge v. Cartledge, 7 W. & S., 394; Boyer v. Smith, 5 W., 55; Stub v. Leis, 7 W., 43.

[7] Hinkle v. Eichelberger, 2 B., 483; McNeil v. Conwell, 7 B., 368.

[8] Longswamp v. Trexler, 8 Sm., 141; and see Keymborg v. Burbridge, 1 J., 535.

been incurred as well by acts of omission as commission, as where there is a suit upon a bail-bond, and a plea of *non est factum*, the sheriff is incompetent to prove the signature.[1] But where the witness himself would have a remedy over in case of such liability being incurred, he is competent; as where an administrator has paid a claim which he may recover back, in a contest before the auditor of his account he is competent to testify in its favor;[2] and when lapse of time or the statute of limitations is a bar to any subsequent suit against the witness, he is competent.[3]

(e.) *Where the Judgment may Serve to Charge the Estate of the Witness or Deprive him of it.*—Where the suit is one concerning land, the title to which the witness has, and the result of the suit would be to fix a charge upon the land, he is incompetent; as, in the case of a *sci. fa.* to revive a judgment, the *terre-tenant*, whose estate might thus be charged with the judgment, is incompetent to testify for the defendant;[4] or a purchaser from the owner of land sued for maintaining a continuing nuisance.[5] But the mere holding under the same title does not, necessarily, exclude the witness, unless the witness's estate may be affected. The relation of landlord and tenant does not preclude a lessee from being a witness for the lessor in an action by him against a trespasser for injury to the reversion.[6] A tenant in common is competent for his co-tenant in an action of ejectment brought by him;[7] and in an action of account-render by one co-tenant against another, as bailiff for him, a third co-tenant is competent for the plaintiff.[8]

[1] Baxter *v.* Graham, 5 W., 418.

[2] Christman *v.* Siegfried, 5 W. & S., 400.

[3] Ludlow v. Ins. Co., 2 S. & R., 119; Unger *v.* Wiggins, 1 R., 331; Levers *v.* Van Buskirk, 4 B., 309; Breitenbach *v.* Houtz, 11 C., 153.

[4] Kuester *v.* Keck, 8 W. & S., 16.

[5] Miller *v.* Frazier, 3 W., 456.

[6] Schnable *v.* Koehler, 4 C., 181; Pennsylvania Salt Manufacturing Company *v.* Neel, 4 Sm., 9.

[7] Bennett *v.* Hethington, 16 S. & R., 193; Kifer *v.* Brenneman, 1 B., 452.

[8] Steffen *v.* Hartzell, 5 Wh., 448.

Interest in Equilibrio.—If the witness has conflicting interests in the result of a suit, and the loss and the gain are even, the interest of the witness is said to be *in equilibrio*, and he is competent at the call of either side. Thus, in an action of ejectment, where both plaintiff and defendant claimed under deed and warranty of the same vendor, his widow was held competent, because the measure of the liability of her husband's estate was exactly the loss which one or other of the parties must suffer;[1] and in a suit by an indorsee against the acceptor, the drawer, to whose own order the draft was drawn, was competent at the call of the plaintiff to prove the signature;[2] so, where a judgment has been opened to let creditors prove that it was fraudulent as to them, the debtor is competent to prove the fraud;[3] so he is in trover by his assignees against a creditor, asserting a lien.[4] In any case, where the witness would be equally liable in either event of the suit, he is competent;[5] and wherever it is impossible to weigh the preponderance of interest, the witness is competent,[6] for the cardinal rule of exclusion is, that the interest must be certain.[7]

Preponderance of Interest.—It very frequently happens that one called as a witness is interested to a certain extent in the success of both sides, and it becomes a question to be determined on which side his greater advantage lies, for in that direction must his interest tend; the measure of his disqualifying interest being the excess of one actual interest over the other. This, in many cases, amounts merely to the costs of the suit in which he is called;

---

[1] Brindle *v.* McIlvaine, 10 S. & R., 282; and see Nessly *v.* Swearingen, Add., 144.

[2] Reid *v.* Geoghegan, 1 M., 204 (D. C.).

[3] Sommer *v.* Sommer, 1 W., 303.

[4] Jacoby et al. *v.* Laussat, 6 S. & R., 300.

[5] Zeigler *v.* Gray, 12 S. & R., 42; Miller *v.* Stem, 2 B., 286; Blewett *v.* Coleman, 4 Wr., 45; Girard F. and M. Ins. Co. *v.* Marr, 10 Wr., 504; Finney's Appeal, 9 Sm., 398.

[6] Potter *v.* Burd, 4 W., 15.

[7] Rees *v.* Livingston, 5 Wr., 113.

as in the case of the tenant for whose rent the goods of a third person have been levied upon, and he has brought replevin for them; under an issue of no rent in arrear, the tenant's interest is, that the landlord may lose his suit, in order that he may not, in addition to the amount of the rent, have the costs of the present suit to pay to the plaintiff.

The drawer of a bill called to prove that it was drawn for his accommodation, in a suit by the holder against the acceptor is liable for the amount of the note to one or other of the parties, whichever way the judgment goes, but in case the acceptor has to pay the note, he will be liable to him for the costs of this suit also, and is incompetent when called by him.[2] So, too, when the maker is called by the indorser in a suit brought against him by the holder.[3] And for the same reason the principal debtor is incompetent for the defendant in a suit on a recognizance for stay of execution.[4] But it is not only the costs which settle the preponderance. It may sometimes be measured in other ways. It may be the greater interest which the witness has in an estate, if his claim is that of legatee rather than under the intestate law in an issue *devisavit vel non*,[5] or his greater interest in one of two estates between which there is a contest.[6] If the interest on the one side is certain, and on the other side uncertain and contingent, this makes a preponderance which disqualifies.[7]

Testimony against Interest.—When one is called to testify against his own interest, if not a party to the record, nor a party to negotiable paper, it is a fact in favor of his credibility; as *Gilbert* says, "He is the best witness that can be against himself."

[1] Rush *v.* Flickwire, 17 S. & R., 82.
[2] Smith *v.* Thorne, 9 W., 144.
[3] Davenport *v.* Freeman, 3 W. & S., 557.
[4] Morrison *v.* Hartman, 2 H., 55.
[5] Dickinson *v.* Dickinson, 11 Sm., 401.
[6] Guldin *v.* Guldin, 10 W. N. C., 395.
[7] Atkinson, Assignee, *v.* Purdy, 2 Cl., 317. This principle is thought to be correct, but it is not clear that this case is a strong authority to maintain it.

The testimony of a witness against his own interest may tend either to charge himself[1] with a debt or claim, to discharge others at the witness's own expense,[2] to decrease a fund in which the witness is entitled to share,[3] or to exonerate his debtor from a claim, at the expense of his own creditors.[4]

[1] Work v. McClay, 2 S. & R., 415; Wolf v. Carothers, 3 S. & R., 240; Hawthorn v. Bronson, 16 S. & R., 269; Comm. Bank v. Wood, 7 W. & S., 89; Hayes v. Gudykunst, 1 J., 221; Brown v. Burk, 1 H., 146; Darlington's Appropriation, Id., 430.

[2] Baird v. Cochran, 4 S. & R., 397; Ralph v. Brown, 3 W. & S., 395; Allentown Bank v. Beck, 13 Wr., 394; Bruner v. Wallace, 8 W. N. C., 199 (C. P.).

[3] King v. Faber, 1 Sm., 388.

[4] McCormac v. Hancock, 2 B., 310; Jones v. Bank North. Lib., 8 Wr., 253.

CHAPTER III.

EXCEPTIONS TO THE RULE OF EXCLUSION ON ACCOUNT OF INTEREST.

Exceptions to the Rule of Exclusion.—Although the rule excluding the testimony of parties and interested persons was supposed to be founded upon the want of integrity on their part, it was nevertheless conceded that in some cases they could be depended upon, or rather that they would have to be depended upon. The cases in which their testimony would always be received were:
1. To prove collateral facts for the information of the court.
2. *Ex necessitate rei.*
3. In the case of agents.
4. In the case of beneficial and religious societies.

1. *To Prove Collateral Facts for the Information of the Court.*—The oath of a party to the record has always been receivable in support of or against a motion made in the progress of a cause;[1] and, indeed, the oath of the party himself was made necessary by statute in numerous cases, as in the case of an appeal from a magistrate's court.

It is to be observed, that these are not cases in which, strictly speaking, the testimony of the party is given; they are mere affidavits with no cross-examination, and are neither introduced before the jury nor at the trial. But the party himself is open to *viva voce* examination, even on the trial of the cause, to identify papers which it is intended to offer in evidence,[2] or a family Bible which has been in the custody of the witness.[3] On the ground

---

[1] Nav. Co. *v.* Diffebach, 1 Y., 367; Bank of Pa. *v.* Hadfeg, 3 Y., 560; Buchanan *v.* Streper, 5 W. N. C., 289 (C. P.).

[2] Lenox, Admr., *v.* De Haas, 2 Y., 37; Standley *v.* Weaver, 2 Y., 256.

[3] Carskadden *v.* Poorman, 10. W., 82.

of the necessities of commerce, too, he is competent to prove his book of original entries, made by himself, for goods sold or work done in a suit for the price of the same against the person charged therewith on the books;[1] but he is not competent to prove the handwriting of another in a book of original entries, even though that other be dead,[2] nor to prove even his own entries in a suit against one who is not the person against whom the entries have been made;[3] yet an administrator was held competent to prove his intestate's book of original entries, it not appearing that any one else was alive who could do so.[4] He has been held competent to identify other articles collaterally brought into the case, though not necessary to a determination of the issue, as a certificate of marriage, or blocks of wood said to have been marked by one of the parties in an action of ejectment.[5] When notice has been served upon the other side to produce papers, a party is competent to prove service of the notice,[6] the party upon whom notice has been served is competent and the proper witness to prove his inability to produce them;[7] and a party is competent generally to prove service of notice of facts collateral to the issue,[8] but not the service of a notice which is the necessary preliminary to a suit.[9] Preparatory to offering a deed in evidence, the party by whom it is to be offered is competent to prove an ineffectual effort to subpœna a subscribing witness,[10] but he is not himself competent to

---

[1] Kaughley v. Brewer, 16 S. & R., 133; Shaw v. Levy, 17 S. & R., 99; Est. Ambrose White, 11 Ph., 100 (O. C.).

[2] Karsper v. Smith, 1 Brown, LIII.; *Cf.* Bank v. Brown, 5 S. & R., 231.

[3] Poultney v. Ross, 1 Dall., 238.

[4] Ash v. Patton, 3 S. & R., 300.

[5] Davis v. Houston, 2 Y., 289; Coxe v. Ewing, 4 Y., 429.

[6] Jordan v. Cooper, 3 S. & R., 564; Siltzell v. Michael, 3 W. & S., 329.

[7] Silliman v. Molloy, 4 Ph., 44.

[8] McCormick v. Crall, 6 W., 207; Union Canal Co. v. Loyd, 4 W. & S., 393.

[9] Crozer v. Leland, 4 Wh., 12; Minor v. Neal, 1 B., 403, *overruling* Kidd v. Riddle, 2 Y., 444.

[10] Douglass v. Sanderson, 1 Y., 15.

prove the execution of the deed;[1] he may prove that a deposition has been properly taken,[2] or that the deponent cannot attend,[3] in order that the deposition may be received in evidence. When a paper has been shown to have once been in the witness's possession, he is competent to prove its loss.[4]

In Diehl v. Emig, 15 Sm., 320, where the actual delivery of a deed to the plaintiff was not proven, although its existence was proven, and the declaration of the grantor that the plaintiff had given him all of her papers to keep, it was said generally, though apparently without much consideration, nor was the actual point raised, that the plaintiff was incompetent to prove the loss of the deed so as to lay the ground for parol proof, which certainly was too broad a statement of the rule not recalling the exceptions, and one not necessary to the decision of the case in hand.

2. *Ex Necessitate Rei.*—It has been said by high authority in this State, TILGHMAN, C. J., that "necessity, either absolute or moral, is sufficient ground for dispensing with the usual rules of evidence."[5] And it was upon this theory that subsequently this same judge held an administrator competent to prove his intestate's book of original entries in a suit by himself as administrator, there appearing to be no one else who could do so. This is the reason given for the admission of secondary evidence generally;[6] but the admission of incompetent witnesses is not the admission of secondary evidence, which is perfectly competent in the absence of the best evidence; it is the admission of that which would not be evidence at all if it were not for the suspension of the rules of exclusion. Neither is it strictly correct to say that necessity alone is in any case sufficient to admit the testimony of a party, or one otherwise in-

---

[1] Peters v. Condron, 2 S. & R., 80.

[2] Black v. Moore, 1 B., 344.

[3] Little's Lessee v. Flora, *cited* 1 Y., 16; Keyser v. Rodgers, 14 Wr., 275.

[4] Meeker v. Jackson, 3 Y., 442; Snyder v. Wolfley, 8 S. & R., 328; Grant v. Levan, 4 B., 427.

[5] Garwood v. Dennis, 4 Binn., 316.   [6] Fox v. Lyon, 3 C., 9.

competent, if by necessity is meant the inability to obtain other testimony, for upon that principle the rules of exclusion would be broken every day, and those cases which have failed for want of competent testimony would be much fewer. What is meant by the rule of admission *ex necessitate rei* is, that in those cases in which from the very *nature* of the case, not from the circumstances, the evidence of a party is the only evidence attainable,—the party is a competent witness to prove those facts. Upon this ground, therefore, the evidence of parties and interested persons is admissible in actions for damages for the loss of articles of wearing apparel intrusted to the defendants, or which they were bound to protect, for the purpose of proving their existence and value;[1] and the privilege has been extended to a wife who was held competent to prove the contents of a trunk on behalf of her husband;[2] but beyond the proof of those things which, *ex necessitate rei*, are within the knowledge of the party alone, the reason of the rule and its operation cease, and it does not extend to the proof of money lost or furniture injured, or to the existence or loss of anything beyond such articles of wearing apparel as are ordinarily in use.[3] So, too, in quite another class of cases the reason of the rule again exists; and it was said by KING, P. J., that, in contested election cases, since the law required that the petitioners should have been voters, and no one can prove a voter's ballot but himself, the petitioner should be a competent witness for that purpose.[4]

3. *Agents.*—All of the exceptions to the rule of exclusion, it will be observed, are founded upon some actual or supposed necessity; and in the case of agents, who, although they may be interested, are permitted to testify in actions to which their principals are parties, the rule is said to exist "for the sake of trade and the

---

[1] Clark *v.* Spence, 10 W., 335; David *v.* Moore, 2 W. & S., 230; Whitesell *v.* Crane, 8 W. & S., 369; County *v.* Leidy, 10 B., 45.

[2] McGill *v.* Rowand, 3 B., 451.

[3] See note 1, *supra*, and Bingham *v.* Rogers, 6 W. & S., 495.

[4] Kneass's Case, 2 Pars., 553.

common usage of business; or, where no other witness is reasonably to be expected."[1] It was soon restricted, however, to include the case of agents dealing as such, who, although the result of the suit against their alleged principals may be to exonerate them personally from the debt or damages for which they are alleged to have rendered the principals responsible, are nevertheless admitted at the call of either the adverse party or their principals to prove their own agency,[2] and also to testify generally,[3] except when their own negligence, or fraud, or tortious conduct is the point at issue. The rule extends to all cases of agency, including that of an attorney for his client, who is competent for his principal,[4] although of course no confidential communication could be imparted without the consent of the client. But when the point at issue is the negligence, or other tortious or fraudulent act of the agent, he is incompetent at the call of either side to exonerate his principal from his own alleged acts,[5] or even those of persons acting for him.[6] The agent's deputy, however, is not himself incompetent in a suit against his principal's principal, as the agent of a sheriff's deputy, in trespass against the sheriff.[7] When one who is really the agent of an undisclosed principal has been dealing as principal, and would be personally liable, if the agency is not proven, in a suit against his principal, he is incompetent to prove his agency at the call of the plaintiff;[8] but, when the position is reversed, in a suit by his

[1] Miller v. Hayman, 1 Y., 24.

[2] McGunnagle v. Thornton, 10 S. & R., 251; Ridgeley v. Dobson, 3 W. & S., 118; Culbertson v. Isett, 2 J., 198.

[3] McDowell v. Simpson, 3 W., 129; Bank v. Beale, 1 W. & S., 227; O. C. v. Woodburn, 7 W. & S., 162; Struthers v. Kendall, 5 Wr., 214.

[4] Linton v. Comm., 10 Wr., 294.

[5] Humphreys v. Reed, 6 Wh., 435; Schuyl. Nav. Co. v. Harris, 5 W. & S., 28; Plumer v. Alexander, 2 J., 81; Loudon Sav. F. Soc. v. Hagerstown Sav. Bank, 12 C., 498; Catawissa RR. Co. v. Armstrong, 13 Wr., 186.

[6] Sheerer v. Lautzerheiser, 6 W., 551; Dorrance v. Comm., 1 H., 160.

[7] Comm. v. Allen, 6 C., 49.

[8] Hickling v. Fitch, 1 M., 208; Meason v. Kaine, 13 Sm., 335.

principal, such an agent is competent when called by him.[1] In order to exclude the testimony of a witness on the ground of negligence in the performance of his agency there must be evidence that the person offered as a witness was acting in the capacity of agent with this duty to perform,[2] and that his negligence is the point at issue.[3] It has been held that the presumption of negligence on the part of an attorney-at-law, to whom has been intrusted the collection of an unpaid note from the maker, in which he has failed, is too remote to disqualify him in a suit by the holder against the indorser.[4]

(4.) *Trustees and Members of Charitable or Religious Societies.*—The trustees of beneficial, charitable, or religious societies who would be personally liable for costs in case of the adverse result of a suit, are nevertheless excepted from the rule of exclusion, on the ground of policy, if not of necessity, if no other personal interest attaches to the result of the suit.[5]

But when the result of the suit would be to charge the members with an assessment for the purpose of paying the claim in suit if recovered,[6] or when the fund in which the members are entitled to share would be diminished by a recovery against the society,[7] the personal interest in the result of the suit is sufficient to exclude.

Privilege of Refusing to Testify.—The fact of being a party or interested person has heretofore been treated wholly as a disability. At common law, however, it was also a privilege extended to the party to the record or one directly interested, which, while it closed his mouth on his own behalf, protected him also from any admissions he should be compelled to make if called by his opponent. The rule was, that one who was actually or substantially a

---

[1] Gilpin *v.* Howell, 5 B., 41.
[2] Dodge *v.* Bache, 2 Pitts, 487.
[3] Smith *v.* Seward, 3 B., 342.
[4] Braine *v.* Spalding, 2 Sm., 247.
[5] Shortz *v.* Unangst, 3 W. & S., 45; Davies *v.* Morris, 5 H., 205; Sorg *v.* First German Cong., 13 Sm., 156.
[6] Wash. Benef. Soc. *v.* Bacher, 8 H., 425.
[7] The Marion Benef. Soc. *v.* Comm., 7 C., 82; S. C., 2 Ph., 129.

party to the cause, could not be compelled by the other side to testify; and to constitute one a party entitled to claim this privilege, it was not necessary that his name be on the record; so that in a suit to which a trustee was a party, the *cestui que trust* would be privileged; or a partner not sued; or the plaintiff in an execution, for levying which the sheriff is sued in trespass;[1] and, when a party testified to his own book of original entries, his opponent was not permitted to examine him as to other matters.[2] But one who was not substantially a party, but was merely interested, could not claim the privilege;[3] moreover, the privilege was merely a personal one belonging to the witness, and if not enforced by him, was no obstacle to the admission of his testimony.[4]

[1] Norman *v.* Norman, 2 Y., 154; Patterson *v.* Hagerman, 2 Y., 163; Taylor *v.* Henderson, 17 S. & R., 453; Welsh *v.* Cooper, 8 B., 217.

[2] Shaw *v.* Levy, 17 S. & R., 99.

[3] Quinlan *v.* Davis, 6 Wh., 169; Ralph *v.* Brown, 3 W. & S., 395; Brewster's Adm. *v.* Sterrett, 8 C., 115.

[4] Quinlan *v.* Davis, 6 Wh., 174.

CHAPTER IV.

HISTORY OF RELEASES.

Removal of Disqualification by Release.—The right of a party to the suit to offer the testimony of one who, although he may have been interested in the result of the suit, had extinguished, or, had received an extinguishment of that interest, either by an assignment or release of it, if it were an expectant right, or a release, if it were an expectant liability, has always been familiar law. Greenleaf says: "The competency of a witness may always be restored by a proper release;" and since the incompetency of a party was based upon interest only, it was immaterial whether the person whose testimony was thus offered was a party or merely an interested person, but in this State a new line of policy was adopted, not in consonance either with the English law or with our own earlier cases. Impressed with the importance of excluding everybody who had an interest in the subject-matter of a suit, the feeling gradually grew up that not only would the testimony be false if the witness were interested at the time it was given, but even if he *had* been interested at one time, and was a party on the record nominally to support that interest; that there was something inherently improper and indelicate in one who was on the record as a party permitting his own testimony to be used in support of the case represented by his name. From this there was still another development: that it was not only improper that one who was nominally a party should give testimony, but that one who had ever been a party to the transaction out of which the suit arose was equally incompetent; and thirdly, a rule once adopted in England, but subsequently overruled there, was enforced here, to wit, that one whose name appeared on negotiable paper was incompetent to impeach it. "We will briefly sketch the origin and progress of this development.

It had been a matter of daily practice for the vendors of land with warranty, to obtain releases from their warrantees, and then they were admitted as fully competent. In 1811 was decided the case of Steele *v.* The Phœnix Ins. Co., 3 Binn., 306. This was an action by William and James Steele upon an insurance policy. The suit was brought to March term, 1805; on the 3d of June following the plaintiffs assigned all of their property to assignees for the benefit of creditors, from whom they received a release in November, 1805. On the morning of the trial a paper was filed in court, declaring that the suit was for the use of the assignees, by whom all of the past and prospective costs of the trial were paid; they also gave to the assignees on the day of the trial a release of all interest in the money to be recovered in the suit, and upon this state of facts offered William Steele, one of the plaintiffs, as a witness; he was admitted, and the question of his competency reserved for the Court in banc, TILGHMAN, C. J., YEATES, and BRACKENRIDGE, JJ. They were unanimously of the opinion that the witness was competent. TILGHMAN, C. J., said that it was clear that he was not interested at the time that his testimony was given, and proceeded: "It is insisted on by the defendants as a peremptory rule of law, that the plaintiff in the action cannot be a witness. . . . . Now what good reason is there why a man's testimony should be excluded, merely because his name is placed on the record as a party to a suit, in which he has no manner of interest. The reason for admitting such evidence is much stronger *here than in England.* In this State we have no Court of Chancery, and therefore the assignee of a chose in action is compelled to bring his action in the name of the assignor; whereas *in England* he may file a bill in equity, in his own name, and thus in some instances obviate the objection arising from the assignor being plaintiff on the record, in case he wants to make use of his testimony;" and after discussing the possibility of fraud in the assignment, of which he saw no evidence in the case before him, he finally stated that he was "satisfied, that the evidence was properly admitted." The rule established in this case was affirmed and reaffirmed many times, and the practice adopted in it became the common practice for the purpose of rendering competent the plaintiffs on the record, the assignments and releases being made both before[1] and after suit brought,[2] so that, indeed, an actual plaintiff in his own right was enabled to assign his claim after suit brought, for the very purpose of rendering himself competent.[3]

It had been said, in Steele v. Phœnix Ins. Co., that if there were fraud in the assignment the court would reject the evidence, but the burden of showing fraud was upon the party objecting to the release. It was here, therefore, that the attack upon the practice was made, and in Post v. Avery, 5 W. & S., 509 (1843), GIBSON, C. J., after stating that the practice of obtaining evidence by this means had been "proved by experience to be intolerably mischievous in its consequences," ruled that "an assignment merely colorable shall not devest the title to make the plaintiff a witness, whatever its legal effect between the parties; and that every assignment is to be deemed colorable when no other motive for it can be made to appear:" in this case the plaintiff had executed an assignment of the cause of action to his son at the trial. In the following year an assignment of all interest in a claim of $2000, alleged to be due to a firm, was made by one partner to the other in consideration of $300, and the assignee, within six days brought suit in the name of the firm to his own use; but, on writ of error, the court held this to be colorable, and the witness incompetent.[4]

---

[1] Wistar v. Walker, 2 Br., 166; Browne v. Weir, 5 S. & R., 401; Fetterman v. Plummer, 9 S. & R., 20.

[2] McEwen v. Gibb, 4 D., 137; Hart v. Heilner, 3 R., 407; Patton v. Ash, 7 S. & R., 116; North v. Turner, 9 S. & R., 244; Willing v. Peters, 12 S. & R., 177; Clement v. Bixler, 3 W., 248; Hoak v. Hoak, 5 W., 80.

[3] Willing v. Peters, 12 S. & R., 177.

[4] Patterson v. Reed, 7 W. & S., 144; Reading Railroad Company v. Johnson, Id., 317.

The retreat thus started culminated in McClelland v. Mahon, 1 B., 365, where it was said, in a PER CURIAM: "He ought, therefore, to have been rejected as a witness, whether his transfer to the equitable plaintiff were real or fictitious. Nor could his testimony be received for purposes of corroboration. . . . . Indeed the time is come when the doctrine in Steel v. The Phœnix Insurance Company must be exploded altogether. The essential interests of justice demand, that the decision in that case be no longer a precedent for anything whatever." It was, therefore, finally established that no one, once beneficially interested, whose name appeared upon the record as a plaintiff, could be a witness. It was but a step to extend the rule from the plaintiff to the defendant, which was done in Given v. Albert, 5 W. &. S., 333, and Wolf v. Finks, 1 B., 435 (1845), where a defendant, one of the makers of a note upon which suit was brought, in whose favor an award unappealed from had been made, and who, at the time of trial, was a certificated bankrupt, was held incompetent to testify on appeal from the award of arbitration taken by one of the other defendants; ROGERS, J., saying: "But the reason for excluding a witness is not on the ground of interest; it arises from considerations of policy, as appears from all the cases."

Having started upon this line, the courts at last began to adopt the theory that the exclusion of parties was not based at all upon the interest which they had in the suit, but upon "the policy of the law."[1] Interested witnesses were excluded by reason of the policy of the law, too, on the ground, that interest tended to warp the conscience, and the policy which would exclude a party, merely as such, presumably would have been founded upon some similar reasoning; but none is given us by the decisions. It is true, that the rule was not adopted without many solemn adjudications and opinions ut-

---

[1] Kirk v. Ewing, 2 B., 453; Parke v. Bird, 3 B., 360; Norris v. Johnston, 5 B. 287; Burrows v. Shultz, 6 B., 325.

terly at variance with it.[1] The cases, however, are found side by side; one judge expressing the opinion that the exclusion of parties is founded solely upon their interest, and, that once extinguished, they are as competent as any one else; another ruling that, whether interested or not is not the question, the policy of the law excludes a party *ipso facto;* until, in the last of the cases before the act of 1869, STRONG, J., said: "And in this state it is apparently settled that in actions on contract at least, a party to the suit is an incompetent witness, though he may be disinterested. I confess I prefer the English doctrine laid down in Worrall v. Jones, but our cases are too numerous and direct to be disregarded."[2]

Meantime the courts were gradually evolving another rule, which grew out of the fact, that the assignment of the mere "policy of the law" was not a sufficient reason for the exclusion of those merely nominal parties who were plaintiffs to use, but who had long before suit brought become *bona fide* assignors of choses in action, with no liability over, and who merely appeared upon the record as nominal parties without a particle of interest, and with no option to prevent the use of their names. Here, although the reason was not framed in this language exactly, there was some fair argument to be made on the ground of inequality against permitting one party to an alleged contract to place himself in a position to maintain it by his own oath, while the lips of the other party to it were sealed, and the rule was adopted that the assignor of a chose in action, who was the original party to the transaction upon which the claim was founded, was incompetent for his assignee in a subsequent suit to maintain it,[3] and this rule

---

[1] Moddewell v. Keever, 8 W. & S., 63; Peters v. Horbach, 4 B., 134; Solms v. McCullough, 5 B., 476; Mevey v. Matthews, 9 B., 112; Rooney v. Campbell, 6 H., 164; Moore v. Weber, 2 Ph., 81.

[2] Swanzey v. Parker, 14 W., 441; and see Malaun's Admr. v. Ammon, 1 Gr., 123; Cambria Iron Company v. Tomb, 12 Wr., 387; Noble v. Laley, 14 Wr., 281.

[3] Patterson v. Reed, 7 W. & S., 144; Reading RR. Co. v. Johnson, Id., 317; Grayson's Appeal, 5 B., 395; Baily v. Knapp, 7 H., 192; Lindsley v. Ma-

was applied as well to suits in which the claim was used as a set-off as to those in which the action was upon the claim itself.[1]

Upon the same principle of inequality one of two defendants, original parties to the contract in suit, was incompetent to qualify himself in any way to testify for the other in a suit against him.[2] Indeed, so strong became the tendency to exclude that one who was no party to the original transaction, but who happened to have been a temporary owner of the chose in action, who before suit brought had parted with his interest *bona fide*, and had not at the time of trial a particle of interest, was nevertheless held incompetent in support of the claim;[3] but these cases were in effect overruled,[4] although Hatz *v.* Snyder seems to have been regarded as authority, to some extent, even so late as Foreman *v.* Ahl, 5 Sm., 325; but the full extent to which it went was unnecessary for the decision of that case.

Parallel with the cases which had developed the rules of exclusion of parties and assignors of choses in action was another line of cases which was based upon a principle enunciated in the case of Walton *v.* Shelly, 1 T., 300, that one whose name appeared on negotiable paper as a party giving credit to it, should under no circumstances, entirely apart from the question of interest, be entitled to discredit it, LORD MANSFIELD saying that it was "of consequence to mankind that no person should hang out false colors to deceive them, by first affixing his signature to a paper, and then afterwards giving testimony to invalidate it." In England this case was overruled not long after by Jordaine *v.* Lash-

lone, 11 H., 24; Schnader *v.* Schnader, 2 C., 384; Loudon Sav. Fd. Soc. *v.* Hagers. Bank, 12 C., 498; Hottenstein's Appeal, 2 Gr., 301; Foreman *v.* Ahl, 5 Sm., 325.

[1] Muirhead *v.* Kirkpatrick, 2 B., 425; Armstrong *v.* Graham, 4 B., 142.

[2] Graves *v.* Griffin, 7 H., 176; Wells *v.* Peck, 11 H., 155.

[3] Clover *v.* Painter, 2 B., 46; Hatz *v.* Snyder, 2 C., 512.

[4] Beaver *v.* Beaver, 11 H., 167; Evans *v.* Dela, 11 C., 451; and see also Orphans' Court *v.* Woodburn, 7 W. & S., 162.

brooke, 7 T. R., 601, and the rule established according to *Greenleaf* was that " the party to any instrument, whether negotiable or not, is a competent witness to prove any fact to which any other witness would be competent to testify." At the same time the rule of Walton *v.* Shelly was distinctly repudiated by many of the States,[1] but in Pennsylvania it was followed, and the subsequent case overruling it was disregarded.[2]

The rule was limited, however, to apply only to negotiable paper actually negotiated in due course of business, and to transactions which took place prior to the negotiation,[3] and it had no application to cases in which the transfer was by parol,[4] or not in the usual course of business, nor to testimony as to facts occurring subsequent to the negotiation,[5] nor facts occurring entirely *dehors* the note,[6] nor where the action was not upon the note itself,[7] and so too as to facts which have no bearing upon the credit to be given to the note itself.[8] And the party to negotiable paper not being otherwise disqualified, was competent to testify in its support.[9] But no one who would be thus excluded was competent himself to show facts which would bring his case within one of

---

[1] Note 2 Sm. Lead. Cases, 141, Hare and Wallace's Ed.

[2] Stille *v.* Lynch, 2 D., 194; Bank of Montgomery *v.* Walker, 9 S. & R., 229; Griffith *v.* Reford, 1 R., 196; Gest *v.* Espy, 2 W., 265; Harrisburg Bank *v.* Forster, 8 W., 304; Harding *v.* Mott, 8 H., 469; Saurman's Exr. *v.* Bodey, 6 Wr., 476; Thompson *v.* Bank of Gettysburg, 3 Gr., 119.

[3] Brown *v.* Downing, 4 S. & R., 494; Hepburn *v.* Cassel, 6 S. & R., 113; O'Brien *v.* Davis, 6 W., 498; Parke *v.* Smith, 4 W. & S., 287; Appleton *v.* Donaldson, 3 B., 381.

[4] O'Brien *v.* Davis, 6 W., 498; Rick *v.* Kelly, 6 C., 527; Columbia Co. I. Co. *v.* Fox, 9 C., 239; Evans *v.* Dela, 11 C., 451.

[5] Mitchell *v.* Conrow, 5 Wh., 572; Appleton *v.* Donaldson, 3 B., 381; Snyder *v.* Wilt, 3 H., 59; Wilt *v.* Suyder, 5 H., 77.

[6] Work *v.* Kase, 10 C., 139.

[7] Wright *v.* Truefitt, 9 B., 507.

[8] Bank *v.* McCalmont, 4 R., 310; Maynard *v.* Nekervis, 9 B., 81.

[9] Bisbing *v.* Graham, 2 H., 14; Scott *v.* Pilling, 2 Ph., 134.

the exceptions to the rule.[1] It was attempted to bring contracts other than those of negotiable paper within the rule, but it was distinctly held not to apply to any other case[2] of contract except a deed, nor was a party to a fraud estopped from proving it.[3]

[1] Barton *v.* Fetherolf, 3 Wr., 279.

[2] Clyde *v.* Clyde, 1 Y., 92; Baring *v.* Shippen, 2 Binn., 154; McFerran *v.* Powers, 1 S. & R., 102; Kronk *v.* Kronk, 4 W. & S., 127; Himblewright *v.* Armstrong, 1 C., 428; McIldowney *v.* Williams, 4 C., 492.

[3] Langer *v.* Felton, 1 R., 141; Sommer *v.* Sommer, 1 W., 303.

CHAPTER V.

WAIVER OF PRIVILEGE AND REMOVAL OF DISABILITY BY RELEASE.

Waiver of Privilege and Disqualification.—It has been said that when the party to the record waived the privilege accorded to him he might be called by the other side; but this occurred, as may be supposed, most infrequently, no one likely to testify against himself would, in all likelihood, be called by his adversary, and no one who would thus be obliged to testify against himself would be at all likely to waive his privilege of remaining mute. It did not infrequently happen, however, that co-plaintiffs or co-defendants were willing to testify against their own interests, and it then became a question whether the waiver of the disqualification by the adverse party and the waiver of the privilege by the witness himself was sufficient, or whether the co-plaintiff or co-defendant might effectively interpose his objections. ROGERS, J., said in Quinlan *v.* Davis, 6 Wh., 174, "When one of several co-plaintiffs comes forward voluntarily, or, when called by the defendant, makes no objection, to disprove the defendant's liability to the demand made upon him, he may be admitted, with the consent of the adverse party, though at the same time, he defeats the claim of those who jointly sue with him;" and so GIBSON, C. J., in Moddewell *v.* Keever, 8 W. & S., 63, "As a party plaintiff; Hamilton was competent to testify against his fellows and himself," and the same opinion was carefully expressed in the District Court by HARE, J., in Moore *v.* Weber, 2 Ph., 81. The same ruling governed in the cases of defendants, who were also held competent against the interests of their co-defendants when called by the plaintiff.[1] But

---

[1] Norman *v.* Norman, 2 Y., 154; Whitehead *v.* Bank, 2 W. & S., 172; Peters *v.* Horbach, 4 B., 134; Solms *v.* McCullough, 5 B., 473; Loudon Sav. Fd. Soc. *v.* Hagerstown Soc., 12 C., 498; Mevey *v.* Matthews, 9 B., 112; Bowen *v.* Burk, 1 H., 146; O'Brien *v.* Vantine, 1 Cl., 210.

eventually, when the theory of exclusion of parties by reason of "the policy of the law" alone, had reached its development, the reasoning of all of these cases became valueless, and it was held as a positive rule of practice that without the consent of all parties to the record no one of them should be competent to testify either for or against his own interest.[1]

The Removal of Disabilities.—The removal of the disability of a person incompetent to be a witness by reason of his interest could always be effected by an assignment or release wherever the rules heretofore laid down did not prevail, that is to say, whenever the person offered was not a party either nominally or actually, nor one of the original parties to the contract or claim in suit, nor one whose name was on negotiable paper which he was called to discredit.[2] When interested in land or a fund which might be affected by the suit, the proper course is for the witness to give an absolute and unqualified release of all such interest to the party on the record who represents that interest; as where under a contract one is interested in land if recovered by plaintiff, he may rescind the agreement and render himself competent;[3] and a *cestui que trust*, who has released all interest in the trust estate, is competent to testify on its behalf.[4] In the case of the stockholder of a corporation who has sold his stock, he is competent for the corporation in an action by or against it.[5] The cases which have been most numerous, however, are those in which persons interested in the estates of decedents have sought to qualify themselves. It was at first held, on the authority of Steele v. The Phœnix Insurance Company,[6] that one interested as legatee of an

[1] Swanzey v. Parker, 14 Wr., 441.
[2] Comm. to Use v. Ohio and Penna. RR. Co., 1 Gr., 348.
[3] McLaughlin v. Shields, 2 J., 283.
[4] Martin v. McCord, 5 W., 493.
[5] Hartman v. Keystone Ins. Co., 9 H., 466; Meighen v. Bank, 1 C., 288; Shoemaker v. Bank, 9 Sm., 79.
[6] *Ante*, p. 49.

estate would be competent to prove the will under which he claimed, if he first assigned all interest without warranty,[1] but subsequently the last preceding case directly on this point, Search's Appeal, 1 H., 108, was overruled *eo nomine*, and with it of course fell those cases on which it was founded. The case by which it was overruled was Haus *v.* Palmer, 9 H., 296, where an issue had been directed to try the validity of an alleged will, but before issue joined, one of the legatees under the alleged will had assigned to another, so that she was not included in the issue at all, and was not beneficially interested; it was held, that although a legatee might renounce, it was not possible to assign his claim so as to become competent, because it gave the witness every advantage of the will, and withal permitted him to justify it by his evidence;[2] but it was admitted that it would be competent for him to release all interest, and thus by declining to be interested, preserve his original competency.[3] When, however, the issue is not upon the validity of the will, but an action is brought by an executor or administrator on behalf of an estate, a legatee or distributee who has been absolutely paid his legacy, or has released[4] or assigned[5] all interest in the verdict is competent. And where the executor or administrator is defendant a legatee or devisee of a distributive share or a distributee may make themselves competent in the same manner.[6] But this could not be done if the proffered witness were himself joined as a party;[7] and if although not nominally a party the witness is beneficially interested so as to be liable for costs, a release unaccompanied by a payment of the past and prospective

---

[1] Kerns *v.* Soxman, 16 S. & R., 315; McIlroy *v.* McIlroy, 1 R., 433; Search's Appeal, 1 H., 108.

[2] Haus *v.* Palmer, 9 H., 296, and see Montgomery *v.* Grant, 7 Sm., 243.

[3] Cornell *v.* Vanartsdalen, 4 B., 364.

[4] Cox *v.* Norton, 1 P. & W., 412; Forrester *v.* Kline, 14 Sm., 29.

[5] Cook *v.* Grant, 16 S. & R., 198; Dellone *v.* Rehmer, 4 W., 9; Steininger *v.* Hoch's Exr., 6 Wr., 432.

[6] Newlin *v.* Newlin, 1 S. & R., 275.

[7] Asay *v.* Hoover, 5 B., 21; Norris *v.* Johnston, Id., 287.

costs is useless.[1] In the case of persons interested in the record as an instrument of evidence their competency may be restored by releases given to them, or by them, as the case may be, as when there is a possible liability over to the party calling the witness either for the whole amount involved[2] in the suit or for the costs alone,[3] and where the plaintiff or defendant may be liable to the witness in the event of his failure in the suit, the release of the witness to him will qualify the witness.[4]

Sometimes there may be a double interest, so that not only is it necessary that a release should be given by the witness, but he should also receive one from the party for whom he is to be called; as in an action by M. against B., a partner of the defendant not sued took a release from him exonerating him from contribution, but was still incompetent because of his interest in the joint funds of the partnership which might be diminished by the suit.[5]

What Constitutes a Good Release.—A seal affixed to a release imparts, as it always does, a consideration, and it is sufficient of itself to make the release effective, but if the instrument is not under seal and no consideration is expressed it is valueless.[6] If the release is a valid instrument in every respect effective, if accepted, "it is sufficient . . . to file the release or deliver it to a third party, for the benefit of the person called to give evidence," BELL, J., in Cameron *v.* Paul, 6 B., 322; the law will presume its acceptance.

---

[1] Montgomery *v.* Grant, 7 Sm., 243.

[2] Lilly *v.* Kitzmiller, 1 Y., 28; Buchanan *v.* Montgomery, 2 Y., 72; Comm. *v.* Watmough, 6 Wh., 117; Bank *v.* Brown, 5 S. & R., 226; McKee *v.* Gilchrist, 3 W., 230; Willard *v.* Wickham, 7 W., 292; Summers *v.* Wallace, 9 W., 161; Myre *v.* Ludwig, 1 B., 47; Cameron *v.* Paul, 6 B., 322; Dayton *v.* Newman, 7 H., 194; Strohecker *v.* Hoffman, 7 H., 223; Roth *v.* Crissy et al., 6 C., 145.

[3] Dickinson College *v.* Church, 1 W. & S., 462; Miller *v.* Stem, 2 J., 383.

[4] Byers *v.* Mullen, 9 W., 266; Ins. Co. *v.* Simmons, 6 C., 299.

[5] Black *v.* Marvin, 2 P. & W., 138.

[6] Schuylkill Nav. Co. *v.* Harris, 5 W. & S., 28.

CHAPTER VI.

PRACTICE.

Matters of Practice.—Having now considered the rules governing the disqualification of witnesses arising from their being parties or persons interested in the result of the suit, it becomes important to observe the proper practice for the purpose of taking advantage of the occasion; and herein we will consider (1) the time at which the objection should be made; (2) the method of bringing it before the court; (3) the character of the objection generally; and (4) other matters of practice.

(1.) *The Time of the Objection.*—The usual and the proper time to object to a witness as incompetent is when he is called to testify, and if the objection is overruled, an exception should at once be taken; but, as sometimes happens, although objection has been made, the party objecting has omitted to take an exception, and finds himself going to the jury with nothing on the record to show error; in that case it is not too late, if he has himself made no use of the testimony for his own purposes, to ask the court to instruct the jury to disregard it, and upon the failure of the court to do so, he may have an exception thereupon.[1] But one disposed to object to a witness on the ground of incompetency may have estopped himself from doing so, as where a plaintiff has been examined before a justice, the counsel of the defendant being present and not objecting, the court will not for this reason reverse on *certiorari*,[2] or when one has in the progress of the trial permitted incompetent evidence to be admitted without objection, and then used it for his own pur-

---

[1] Armstrong *v.* Graham, 4 R., 142.
[2] Stewart *v.* Thompson, 2 Ash., 120; Perot *v.* Harley, 1 Brews., 407.

poses in the course of the argument, it is then too late to request the court to withdraw it.[1]

It may happen that the adverse party is not aware of a witness's interest, and that it is not shown in any way until subsequent testimony in the cause has been given; in such a case the proper course is to move the court then, when the interest is first discovered, to strike out the testimony; or the party objecting may, if he has made no use of the testimony in his argument, request the court to instruct the jury to disregard it;[2] otherwise the court will not reverse on appeal: this rule obtains as well in equitable proceedings where evidence has been taken before an auditor or master.[3] If an ineffectual objection has been made at one period of the trial, and subsequent facts are brought to light which might render it effectual, if the adverse party desires to avail himself of the error in admitting the testimony he must renew his objection, for the court will consider the error as of the time when the objection was made, and hold it to be error only when it appears to have been such at that time.[4] On the other hand, if the court has erroneously excluded a competent witness, and subsequently in the course of the trial the objection is withdrawn, it is competent for him then to be called, and if the party desiring his evidence omit to do so, his original exclusion affords no ground for reversal on writ of error.[5]

(2.) *Method of Bringing the Objection Before the Court.*— When the facts showing the relation which a person offered as a witness bears to the suit, either as a party or one interested in the issue, are all admitted by the parties, the question of his admission

---

[1] Rees *v.* Livingston, 5 Wr., 113; McInroy *v.* Dyer, 11 Wr., 118.

[2] Bank *v.* Wikoff, 2 Y., 39; Lessee of Pollock *v.* Gillespie, Id., 129; Evans *v.* Breban, 2 Ph., 23 (D. C.); Rees *v.* Livingston, 5 Wr., 113; Steamboat Dictator *v.* Heath, 6 Sm., 290; Robinson *v.* Buck, 21 Sm., 386 (February, 1872).

[3] Jones's Appeal, 12 Sm., 324.

[4] Chase *v.* Goldsborough, 1 Ph., 179 (D. C., SHARSWOOD, P. J.).

[5] Small *v.* Jones, 6 W. & S., 122.

is simply one for the determination of the court.¹ When the facts are not apparent, however, and not admitted, there are two methods of bringing them to the notice of the court: first, that of calling the witness upon his *voir dire ;* second, that of proving his interest by extrinsic evidence ;² but both methods can not be pursued at the same time. If no interest is disclosed by the witness in his examination upon his *voir dire,* it is not competent for the party objecting to prove it *aliunde ;*³ but if on his *voir dire* the proffered witness is himself unable to say whether he is interested or not, then the party objecting may prove his interest by evidence *aliunde.*⁴ If after examination upon his *voir dire* no interest has been disclosed, but it subsequently appears in the course of his testimony that he is really interested, the court should reject the witness or withdraw his evidence if requested in time to do so,⁵ and it would seem that this would be the proper practice, too, if the evidence *aliunde* of the side by whom he was called should disclose the same fact.⁶ If a witness has been admitted under objection on the ground of interest, but the party objecting proceeds to cross-examine him, by which it is shown that the interest, whatever it may have been, has been removed, the adverse party cannot object to this result of his cross-examination, and the admission of the witness will not be held to be error.⁷

Where the witness has been examined upon his *voir dire,* the interest must clearly appear in order to render it proper for the court to reject his testimony.⁸ Where a witness has been exam-

¹ Hart *v.* Heilner, 3 R., 407 ; Lyon *v.* Daniels et al., 2 H., 197.

² Mifflin *v.* Bingham, 1 Dall., 294; Vincent *v.* Lessee of Huff, 4 S. & R., 298 ; Gordon *v.* Bowers, 4 H., 230.

³ Mifflin *v.* Bingham, 1 Dall., 294, and note (*a*); Schnader *v.* Schnader, 2 C., 384.

⁴ Shannon *v.* Comm., 8 S. & R., 444; Galbraith *v.* Galbraith, 6 W., 112.

⁵ Davis *v.* Barr, 9 S. & R., 137 ; Armstrong *v.* Graham, 4 B., 142.

⁶ Chase *v.* Goldsborough, 1 Ph., 179 (D. C.).

⁷ Haynes *v.* Hunsicker, 2 C., 58.

⁸ Smith *v.* Moore, 2 Ph., 114 (D. C.) ; Dunlap *v.* Smith, 5 Ph., 69 (D. C.)

ined upon his *voir dire* by the adverse party, and betrayed an apparent interest, it is proper for the party for whom he is called to cross-examine him so as to bring out facts not before disclosed, and thus show him to be disinterested;[1] but a witness not called upon his *voir dire* is not competent to purge himself of interest appearing *prima facie*,[2] or an apparent interest once shown by evidence *aliunde*,[3] and this is so whether the question is decided by the court alone, or, upon a doubt as to the facts, it is left to the jury.[4] On the other hand, the adverse party cannot, after giving evidence *aliunde*, call him upon his *voir dire* to support it.[5]

But the court is not bound to determine questions of fact upon which competency depends when the evidence with regard to the existence of interest is before the court, but the fact of interest existing at all is in doubt; it is proper for the court to admit the testimony of the witness and instruct the jury to find the fact, and if the witness is interested to discard his testimony.[6]

(3.) *Character of the Objection.*—On writ of error, assigning for error the admission or rejection of incompetent witnesses, the presumption is, of course, always in favor of the ruling of the court below. The facts upon which the objection to the admission of a witness is based, as well as the ground of the objection, must appear,[7] and when the error assigned is the rejection of a witness on the ground of interest, the Supreme Court will not

---

[1] Blackstone v. Leidy, 7 H., 335.

[2] Griffith v. Reford, 1 R., 196; Thomas v. Brady, 10 B., 164; Banks v. Clegg, 2 H., 390; Pitts. Coal Co. v. Foster, 9 Sm., 365.

[3] Vincent v. Lessee of Huff, 4 S. & R., 298; Gordon v. Bowers, 4 H., 226; Anderson v. Young's Exrs., 9 H., 443.

[4] Gordon v. Bowers, *supra.*

[5] Peiffer v. Lytle, 8 Sm., 386.

[6] Hart v. Heilner, 3 R., 407; Gordon v. Bowers, 4 H., 226; Trego v. Huzzard, 7 H., 441; Haynes v. Hunsicker, 2 C., 58; Rees v. Livingston, 5 Wr., 113; Lee v. Welsh, 1 W. N. C., 453 (May, 1875).

[7] Snyder v. May & Klose, 7 H., 235; Plank Road Co. v. Ramage, 8 H., 95; Cullum v. Wagstaff, 12 Wr., 300; King v. Faber, 1 Sm. 387.

reverse unless the facts appear upon the record so plainly as to show this to have been error.[1] If only a general objection to a deposition,[2] or an offer of evidence[3] is made and overruled, and any part is admissible, the Supreme Court will not reverse because of its admission, and on the other hand, when any part of it is inadmissible, and it is offered as a whole, there will be no reversal because of its exclusion.[4]

Where the evidence is admissible in one aspect of the case and not in another, it is proper for the court to admit it and control its effect by instructions to the jury;[5] if a specific reason for objection is assigned, the court will not permit the plaintiff in error to travel outside the reason assigned to the court as it appears in the bill of exceptions.[6]

(4.) *Other Matters of Practice.*—A witness may be competent to prove one fact in a case and not another. If the point at issue does not involve the interest of the witness he is competent, or if the point upon which his interest hangs is admitted.[7]

The effect of permitting an incompetent witness to testify in proceedings in equity is not as it would be at common law, ground for reversing the entire decree. If the effect of the evidence is merely to corroborate that which has already been proven by competent testimony, or if the evidence relates to but special items of an account, it may be that the decree will nevertheless be affirmed, or only corrected as to the items affected by the incompetent testi-

---

[1] McCaskey v. Graff, 11 H., 321; Lothrop v. Wightman, 5 Wr., 297; Lahey v. Heenan, 31 Sm., 185 (3 W. N. C., 181).

[2] Peters v. Horbach, 4 B., 134; Batdorff v. Farmers' Nat. Bank, 11 Sm., 179; Bickham v. Smith, 12 Sm., 45; Patterson v. Fay, 1 Ph., 473.

[3] Cullum v. Wagstaff, *supra;* Garsed v. Turner, 21 Sm., 56; Robinson v. Buck, Id., 386; Laubach v. Laubach, 23 Sm., 387.

[4] Sennett v. Johnston, 9 B., 335; Wharton v. Douglass, 26 Sm., 273.

[5] Marshall v. Bobst, 1 Pitts., 137.

[6] Drexel v. Man, 6 W. & S., 343.

[7] Ash v. Patton, 3 S. & R., 300; Gillespie v. Goddard, 1 Pitts., 306

mony.¹ In the case of an auditor's report, unless it is clearly shown that he was led into some specific error by the incompetent evidence, a decree confirming it will be allowed to stand.²

Where a witness has been objected to as incompetent, but admitted subject to the right to exclude his testimony, it is not sufficient for the judge to charge that "under *all* the evidence in the case the plaintiff cannot recover, and their verdict must be for the defendant;" it is the duty of the court to charge expressly on the competency of the witness, if he is inadmissible.³

[1] Sawtelle's Appeal, 3 N., 306, 4 W. N. C., 361; Breneman's Est., 15 Sm., 298; *Cf*. Bank *v.* Downing, 4 S. & R., 494.

[2] Bierly's Appeal, 3 W. N. C., 210 (May, 1876).

[3] Ross *v.* Espy, 16 Sm., 481.

PART II.

LEGISLATION AND ITS RESULTS.

CHAPTER I.

EARLY LEGISLATION.

WE have seen what are the rules of the common law in this State with regard to the competency of witnesses unaffected entirely by statute, we have briefly glanced at the development of the principles originally governing the subject, and the result is, or ought to be, a fair statement of the law as it was, and still is, in all those cases in which the acts of Assembly do not apply. We have seen the greatest diversity of opinion on the part of the bench as to what the law on the subject really has been, due on the one hand to the desire to escape from rules which both legislature and judiciary began to recognize as purely artificial, and on the other to that intense conservatism, so characteristic of the profession, which would not only not give way one jot from the settled law, but even insisted upon pushing its conclusions still further. In the main, however, it may unquestionably be said, that for the past one hundred years the tendency of both the judicial and legislative mind in England and in this country has been undergoing a change in favor of a more untrammelled method of arriving at the truth. In England so early as Lord Hardwicke's and Lord Mansfield's time the tendency was apparent; the former said, in Rex *v.* Bray, 1 Cas. Temp. Ld. Hard., 360, "Whenever an objection of this sort is made at *Nisi Prius* before me I am always inclined to restrain it to the credit, rather than to the competency of the witness, because it tends to let in light to the cause;" and Lord Mansfield said, in Walton *v.* Shelly, 1 T. R., 300: "The old cases upon the competency of witnesses have gone upon very subtle grounds. But of late years the courts have endeavored, as far as possible, consistent with those authorities, to let the objection go to the *credit* rather than the *competency* of a witness."

In this State the first break made by legislation was based upon an extension of the rule of admission arising *ex necessitate rei*, and its application in one case was secured by the act of 1705,[1] by which the mother of a bastard child, being a single woman, was made competent to give evidence in an action against the father, although if convicted in it he was made to pay her lying-in expenses, and to give bond for the maintenance of the child. Thirteen years after the owner of stolen goods was made competent to testify in the prosecution of the thief.[2] After a long interval the now awakened spirit of reform took shape again in a series of special acts, the first of which, to make more effective the prosecution of offenders against the Conestoga Fishing Act, although it was a *qui tam* action, provided that the prosecutor should be competent; and then followed a general act and a series of special acts intended to overcome the inconvenience occasioned in the case of the inhabitants of taxable districts, where a penalty or poor rate could not be collected, because the persons most capable of giving testimony were rated taxpayers; and the settlement of a pauper must go unproved, because in the eye of the law all of the inhabitants of each county to whom he was ascribed were interested in having the expense of his support saddled upon their neighbors. The preamble of the act of April 3d, 1794,[4] puts the case briefly: "Whereas, it appears that great inconveniences arise from the non-admission of the testimony, in cases respecting the settlement of paupers, of persons inhabiting either of the townships concerned, inasmuch as it frequently excludes the best possible light and evidence the nature of the case admits;" therefore, the courts are authorized to admit every otherwise competent person, notwithstanding he or she might be an inhabitant of the city, borough, etc., concerned. The act of

---

[1] 1 Sm. Laws, 27–8.
[2] Act of May 31st, 1718, 1 Sm., 123.
[3] Act of Oct. 4th, 1788, 2 Sm. Laws, 461.
[4] 3 Sm. Laws, 126.

April 11th, 1799,[1] provided that no freeman of the city of Philadelphia, or of any incorporated town or borough, should be incompetent to testify in actions for fines, penalties, and forfeitures to be recovered by the said city, town, or borough, except paupers, for whose benefit such fines might be expended. From this time on a constant succession of special acts, exonerating the inhabitants of boroughs and counties from disability on account of interest in actions brought by the corporate authorities or the overseers of the poor, follow each other through the statute-books, for which were subsequently substituted a series of provisions tacked on to almost every act of incorporation of a new city or borough, by which the competency of its inhabitants as witnesses in such cases was secured.[2] Finally the culmination of this phase of the enabling legislation was reached in the act of February 19th, 1840,[3] which provided that no one should be excluded in any action in which any borough, county, etc., or incorporated district had an interest, by reason of being an officer, or subject to the payment of taxes, or liable to any expense or penalty in the said action.[4] Meantime the act of March 29th, 1832, § 56,[5] provided that "the Orphans' Court, or any auditor appointed by them, shall have power to examine, on oath or affirmation, any of the parties to any proceedings instituted in such court respecting any matter in dispute in such proceedings," thereby extending the jurisdiction of the Orphans' Court to that power ordinarily possessed by courts of equity, of obtaining the

---

[1] 3 Sm. Laws, 390.

[2] No less than twenty-five or thirty such acts and provisos are readily found in the volumes of Smith's Laws. See also McFarland v. Comm., 12 S. & R., 279; Thornbury v. Adams Co., 12 S. & R., 110.

[3] P. L., 52; and see act of May 8th, 1854, § 51; P. L., 629; Purd. Dig., Edition of 1862, pp. 424–5.

[4] Wilson v. Clarion Co., 2 B., 17; Cannell v. Crawford Co., 9 Sm., 196; and see act of April 16th, 1840, § 6; Purd. (1841), 404; Barnet v. School Directors, 6 W. & S., 46.

[5] Purdon's Dig., 1109, § 48.

evidence of parties themselves, if in the opinion of the court it were absolutely necessary.[1] This act was not intended, however, to enable parties to testify on their own behalf, but to render them liable to be called in the discretion of the court.[2]

[1] Iturbide's Est., 1 W. N. C., 316 (O. C.).
[2] Mylin's Est., 7 W., 64; Brencman's Est., 15 Sm., 298; Est. of Jac. Hyneman, 11 Ph., 135 (O. C.).

CHAPTER II.

THE ACTS OF 1865 AND 1867.

The Acts of March 27th, 1865.—Of the acts which may be said to belong to the last series of acts upon this subject, two passed March 27th, 1865, one rendering competent executors, administrators, and guardians in their own cases, the other giving the right to call adverse parties, are the first in order. They will be examined separately.

As we have seen, the only interest which persons acting in fiduciary capacities had in causes brought on behalf of or against the estates which they represented was a personal liability for costs, coupled possibly with an increase or diminution of commissions. This interest was almost purely theoretical, so far as the costs were concerned, for they rarely came out of their own pockets, and if they did, were pretty sure to be reimbursed immediately out of the estates of the beneficiaries, who nevertheless were subjected to a possible failure of justice in consequence of the exclusion of the very persons who in all likelihood had the best acquaintance with the facts, without a controlling interest to govern their statement of them.

To the relief of the beneficiaries, therefore, came the Act of March 27th, 1865, § 1, P. L., 38,[1] providing that

"**In all trials and judicial proceedings, an executor, administrator, trustee, or other person acting in a fiduciary or representative character, although a party to the proceeding, not having any interest in the subject-matter of controversy, may be examined as a witness, and the right to claim commissions or compensation shall not be deemed or taken to be**

---

[1] Purdon's Dig., 623, pl. 12.

an interest disqualifying such person from being examined as any other witness."

This act was first recognized in *Cox* v. *McKean*, 6 Sm., 243 (Nov., 1867), in which assumpsit was brought by an administrator to recover money alleged to have been received from the deceased, and he was permitted to testify; and in *Lecky* v. *Cunningham*, 6 Sm., 371 (Jan., 1868), the testimony of an executor was admitted to prove a will in a feigned issue in which he was a party plaintiff. In *Richter* v. *Cummings*, 10 Sm., 441 (Feb., 1869), a guardian, party to a suit was admitted as a witness on his own behalf, THOMPSON, C. J., saying: "It was to change the policy of the law which forbids parties to the record, although they might not be personally interested, from being witnesses, that the Act of 1865 was passed. It is a remedial act and to be liberally expounded."[1] In keeping with this theory of a liberal interpretation it had been held in *Cox* v. *McKean*, *supra*, that when the plaintiff had shown the defendant to be in point of fact a trustee of money which had come into his hands, although not nominally so, he became *ipso facto* a competent witness under the act. Presumably he would not be competent to testify to facts in denial of his trust, but recognizing that, he would be admissible to give testimony exonerating him from its responsibilities. Little opportunity for questionable construction of this act could or did arise, however, before subsequent legislation removed the possibility of it.

By another act of the same date[2] it was enacted as follows:

"**Any party in any civil action or proceeding, whether at law or in equity, may compel any adverse party, or person, for whose immediate and adverse benefit such action or proceeding is instituted, prosecuted, or defended, to testify as a witness in his behalf in the same manner and subject to the same rules as other witnesses;** *Provided, however,* **That no**

---

[1] See also Vidal's Appeal, 7 W. N. C., 159 (1879).
[2] Act March 27th, 1865, § 1, P. L., 38; Purdon's Dig., 624, pl. 13.

party shall be allowed to compel an answer to a bill of discovery from an adverse party, and also to compel him to testify."

1. *Where a party has taken the testimony of his adversary under the act of 1865, either by deposition or at the time of trial, he has rendered him competent for all purposes in the same trial, or in a subsequent trial of the same issue between the same parties;* but,

2. *The credibility thus acquired is lost by the death of the party who has called his adversary.*

(1.) The object of the act clearly was to remove the privilege which a party to the suit enjoyed of not being liable to affect his own case adversely by his own testimony, unwillingly elicited;[1] but it only enabled his adversary to call him as he would any other witness; he was confined to the same methods of examination, and was as much bound by his testimony as by that of any other witness. It was a precarious right, which parties doubtless availed themselves of very cautiously, and the effect of its use was soon tested. In *Seip* v. *Storch*, 2 Sm., 210 (March, 1867), which was *assumpsit* by Storch against Seip, the defendant, whose defence was a change in the contract, called the plaintiff to prove other parts of his case, and rested; in rebuttal, plaintiff's counsel called the plaintiff to prove that there was no change in the contract, and under objection and exception taken by defendant he was admitted; the verdict and judgment were for plaintiff. On writ of error by the defendant, READ, J., relying particularly upon *Floyd* v. *Bovard*, 6 W. & S., 75, said: "In construing, therefore, the remedial act of 27th March, 1865, P. L., 38, we must apply the well-established principle, that, if a party puts an incompetent witness on the stand, by exercising any power which he possesses over him, he makes him an entirely competent witness in the cause, to be used as such by either party. The learned judge was entirely right, and the judgment is affirmed." The same question, under a different form,

---

[1] See Iturbide's Est., 1 W. N. C., 316 (O. C.).

was raised the next year in *O'Connor* v. *American Iron Co.*, 6 Sm., 234 (Jan., 1868), where the defendant, O'Connor, under the act had taken the deposition of the president of the iron company, plaintiff, and had filed it, but did not offer it in evidence on the trial. The plaintiff requested the court to require the defendants to read the deposition, but this the court declined to do; thereupon the plaintiffs themselves offered it in evidence in rebuttal, under exceptions taken by the defendant. On writ of error, READ, J., said: "Such a deposition of a disinterested witness would clearly have been evidence for either party, . . . and we think the case of Seip *v.* Storch covers the present case."

Both of these cases were affirmed in *Bennett* v. *Williams*, 7 Sm., 404 (April, 1868), where the deposition of the defendant had been taken by the plaintiff under a rule of court requiring the deposition to be filed within a specified time; but it was not filed, and the court refused at the trial to compel the plaintiff to file it. This was held to be error; but no opinion was expressed by the court on another point, whether, the deposition not being forthcoming, it was competent for the defendant to prove that it had been taken, and then offer himself as a witness on his own behalf; however, this was squarely decided in *Forrester* v. *Kline*, 14 Sm., 29 (Feb., 1870), where it was proposed to prove by one of the arbitrators, from whose award an appeal was taken, that one of the defendants had been examined before them, and the court, SHARSWOOD, J., held that it was error to have refused this offer. At the same time it was held, that the notes of testimony, or a deposition taken before the arbitrators, would not have been evidence without proof of the death of the witness, the case before the arbitrators being regarded as a different case from that before the court. The act was referred to, but was not deemed necessary to the decision of the case in *Wolf* v. *Batchelder*, 6 Sm., 87 (Oct., 1867).

(2.) *Credibility Lost by Death of Party Calling.*—This credit which the party to the action may give his adversary is transitory; it does not survive the party himself by whom the waiver was made. In *Menges* v. *Eyster*, 35 Leg. Int., 421 (Oct., 1878), a bill in equity was filed by Menges in his lifetime against Porter Eyster and others. An examiner was appointed, and the complainant called Eyster under the act of 1865; afterward the complainant died, and his administrator was substituted. A feigned issue was ordered by the court to try a question of partnership which was in dispute. At the trial the defendant, Porter Eyster, offered to testify on his own behalf. He was not within the legislation of 1869, but it was urged that under the authority of *Seip* v. *Storch* and *Forrester* v. *Kline*,[1] he had been rendered competent by his testimony before the examiner. AGNEW, C. J., said: "By the decision referred to in Forrester *v.* Kline, under the Act of 1865, the competency of the witness, it is evident, depends on the call of his opponent. . . . . . Here the party to the feigned issue is the administrator of Solomon Menges, and he does not call but objects to the witness. Literally the case is not within the Act of 1865. But he was called by Menges himself in his lifetime, and this, it is said, stamps him with credi[ta]bility, and Forrester *v.* Kline and other cases there held the consequence to be that he is thereby rendered competent. . . . . Menges, the deceased party, no longer represents the case, but it is represented by a legal substitute, who holds the estate for creditors and others. Menges himself knew all the facts, and how far he might run the risk of calling his adversary. If the testimony disappointed him, he knew how and by whom to contradict it, what qualifying facts he could prove, and what other witnesses could be called. Therefore, when he called his adversary before the examiner, he ran the risk, and must take the consequences. But when he died the situation was wholly changed. True, the admission of the credibility of the witness remained, but this did not supply the want of equality, which necessarily expired upon the death of the party. Now there is only a substitute in law, who is not presumed to know, and probably does not know,

---

[1] *Supra.*

the facts and circumstances necessary to be brought to meet the testimony of the living adversary. He must fight a battle altogether unequal, while his adversary has the cause in his own hands. Hence the exception in the Act of 1869 is wholly inconsistent in purpose and effect with the interpretation of the Act of 1865, which enables the defendant to testify in his own behalf when once called by his adversary. It is the *party* in the action or proceeding who may *compel* his adversary to testify. It is he who while alive knows the risk and is presumed to take it. But he is dead, and a new party intervenes, who, as a trustee, has no right to yield up the right of others, and when the very inequality supervenes which the exception in the Act of 1869 was intended to remove, the case is not within the reason of the decisions upon the Act of 1865, and should not be governed by them."

It was said, in *Forrester* v. *Kline* (14 Sm., 29, *supra*), that the notes of testimony would not be evidence without proof of the death of the party by whom the testimony was given. From this the presumption is that they would be evidence if the party calling were alive and the witness dead; but, whether or not, when both parties are dead, this would be the case, has never been decided. From the ruling in *Menges v. Eyster*, it would seem more reasonable to hold that before the act of 1869 made both parties competent for themselves, the death of the party calling would have taken away the credibility of the notes, or the deposition, as well as that of the party himself. Since that act, however, the deposition of a party taken on his own behalf is held competent, notwithstanding the death of his adversary, because it is within the power of both parties to perpetuate their testimony if they desire to do so,[1] and there would seem to be, therefore, no longer any reason to exclude the testimony or deposition of a party called by his adversary.[2]

It may here be properly observed that it has just been decided

---

[1] *Postea*, 148.

[2] *Cf.* Allum *v.* Carroll, 17 Sm., 68 (January, 1871), *postea*, p. 81.

that this act has not been affected by the subsequent act of 1869. *Ash* v. *Guie*, 10 W. N. C., 198 (May, 1881).

Definition of "**an adverse party or person for whose immediate and adverse benefit such action or proceeding is instituted, prosecuted, or defended.**"

An adverse party or person, for whose immediate and adverse benefit such action or proceeding is instituted, prosecuted, or defended, is a person who, by reason of being actually or substantially a party, was, before the act, privileged from testifying, and whose interest, if any, is adverse also.

In *Hogeboom's Exr.* v. *Gibbs, Sterrett & Co.*, 7 N., 235 (Jan., 1879), assumpsit was brought by Gibbs, Sterrett *et al.*, against J. C. Hogeboom, executor of Henry Hogeboom, deceased, for a debt alleged to have been contracted by the deceased, M. H. Philip, and G. J. Sherman, as partners. At the trial, the deposition of Philip was offered in evidence by the plaintiff, *inter alia*, to prove the partnership. In the Supreme Court, PAXSON, J., said: "The witness Philip being incompetent on the ground of interest, he was not made competent by the Act of 27th March, 1865, Pamph. L., 38; Purdon, 624, pl. 13, for the reason that he is neither an adverse party on the record, nor a person for whose immediate and adverse benefit such action was instituted, prosecuted, or defended."

The evident purpose of the act was to remove the *privilege* of refusing to testify, which theretofore existed, and we have already seen that this privilege could only be claimed by those who were actually or substantially parties, although their names need not be upon the record.[1] In all other cases the interest of the witness afforded him no privilege when called to testify against his own interest, and it therefore required no legislation to enable him to be called for that purpose. This being clearly the purpose of the

[1] *Ante*, p. 46.

act, *a fortiori*, words used to take away a privilege arising from interest, are not to be construed as conferring one also, which would be the case, if it were used to obtain testimony from a witness interested on behalf of a person calling him. It will be observed that the act would have applied in the case cited, had the witness, Philip, been called merely to sustain the plaintiff's claim against the firm, for in that case he would have been called to testify against his interest.

In a very recent case, the witness was actually an adverse party on the record, but not in reality. *Guldin* v. *Guldin*, 10 W. N. C., 395 (March, 1881), was a suit brought by one administrator against another; the defendant was a distributee under both estates, but his interest in that represented by the plaintiff preponderated; he was called by the plaintiff, but on writ of error held incompetent. The conclusion to be drawn from the reason of the law, as well as from these cases, is, that one whose *interest* is with the party calling, is not "adverse" within the meaning of the act, and it is immaterial that his position on the record may be adverse, if, in reality, his interest is not so.

In the opinion of the last cited case there is a *dictum* to the effect that the language of the act "applies to a real party, and not to one who sues or is sued as the representative merely;" but, if the representative is not interested on behalf of his nominal adversary, why should not the act apply as well to him as to any other party who claims the privilege of refusing to testify? Unless, indeed, it is understood that the other act of the same date, which removed his incompetency, took away the privilege also; but that was an enabling act, and it is not probable that this was its result; the very fact of his previous incompetency shows him to have been in deed, as well as in name, an "adverse party."

In *O'Rourke* v. *McGrath*, 1 Brews., 302 (Jan., 1867), an attempt was made to bring the wife of a party to the suit within the spirit, if not the letter, of the act, but this construction was repudiated.

It has also been held in a lower court that neither husband nor wife can be called by the other in proceedings for divorce.[1]

Acts of March 28th and April 10th, 1867.—Still hesitating, but always tending in the same direction, the legislature passed the act of March 27th, 1867, § 1, P. L., 47,[2] permitting a defendant in ejectment, who disclaims and has paid or given security for costs accrued, to be a competent witness for either plaintiff or defendant, and its supplement of April 10th, 1867, § 1, P. L., 60,[3] rendering co-plaintiffs or co-defendants of parties compelled to testify under the act of 1865, competent also. (For the text of the acts, *vide* Appendix.)

These acts have received but little attention, owing to the much more important legislation which so soon followed. Upon the construction of the former there seems to be no case at all, but that of April 10th was directly ruled upon in *Allum* v. *Carroll*, 17 Sm., 68 (January, 1871), where, at a hearing before arbitrators, one of several defendants had been called by their adversary, and under this act the testimony of another of the defendants was taken on his own behalf. At the time of the trial both the plaintiff and the defendant whom he had called were dead. The defendants offered as a witness the other defendant who had testified; he being excluded, they offered his testimony taken before the arbitrators, and it was received by the court, but on writ of error it was held to be incompetent, AGNEW, J., saying: "McKenna's testimony was made competent before the arbitrators, not by being called by the plaintiff, and his credibility thus indorsed by him, but by the calling of Thomas Carroll, a co-defendant. . . . Carroll being dead, the plaintiff was not bound to call either of the other defendants, and in fact did not. . . The plaintiff had not indorsed his credibility, and had not chosen that he should be heard alone.

---

[1] Bronson *v.* Bronson, 8 Ph., 261 (C. P., 1871). But see *postea*, p. 140, for a discussion of this decision.

[2] Purdon's Dig., 624, pl. 14. [3] Purdon's Dig., 624, pl. 15.

His former testimony was not more competent than his present testimony, and that the judge had properly excluded." In those cases in which the act of 1869 does not apply, this act is, of course, still operative; but, where at the time that the testimony was taken, all parties and interested persons were competent under the act, the rule of this case does not apply, and the testimony of any defendant taken by virtue of the act, at a time when he was competent, may be offered subsequently, as that of any other witness.

As was to be expected, this course of legislation was only preliminary to a much more general removal of disabilities. While the legislature of this State had been thus delicately approaching the real question which lay at the bottom of all the dissatisfaction, of which these acts were the mere exponents, England, the Federal Government, and many of the other States had taken it in hand, and with greater or less success disposed of it effectually. It is true, that very much the same caution was observed in dealing with the subject that is noticeable here, but in most cases the sense of security in removing the disability seems to have grown more rapidly than it did with us. In 1843, in England, Lord Denman's Act was passed, declaring that neither crime nor interest should render a person incompetent except in the case of parties and those for whose immediate and individual behalf the action was brought or defended, and the husband or wife of such person, and excluding wills from the effect of the act.

In 1850 (Act 14 and 15 Vict., c. 99) the *proviso* was removed so as to leave as the only grounds of incompetency in civil proceedings in England—defect of understanding, defect of religious principles, and the fact of being party to proceedings instituted in consequence of adultery or breach of promise, or the husband or wife of such a party; with this last exception on the score of interest and public policy, neither infamy nor interest any longer remained as a ground of incompetency. Shortly after, parties, their wives, and all other persons were made competent witnesses on either side in the county courts.[1] In the various States a like caution was sometimes observable, but the tendency of all the legislation was in the same direction. In some cases a bold sweep was made, and "neither crime nor interest" was permitted to exclude; in others the incompetency from infamy was limited to conviction for perjury or subornation of perjury; and in others, again, all felonies were retained as infamous crimes, the conviction for which would render the witness incompetent. In some States husband and wife were permitted to testify both for and against each other generally, in others certain cases were excepted from this general rule: in all confidential communications between husband and wife were protected, and sometimes special exceptions were made in favor of other confidential relations, as attorney and client, priest and parishioner, or physician and patient. As in England the removal of the disqualification of parties and interested persons was gradual, so here, in some States, the experiment was first made by the admission of interested persons, but not of parties, or by the admission of parties, with the requirement of an additional witness to corroborate, to render such testimony available. In many cases where both parties and interested persons were admitted generally, special exceptions were made in those cases in which one of the parties to a transaction was dead or had become insane, in which case the other party representing an interest adverse to that of the deceased or insane person was incompetent to testify as to that transaction.

In 1864 the act of Congress was passed which provided that in civil actions there should be no exclusion of any one "because he is a party to or interested in the issue tried." This act must have brought home to the bench and bar of all the States this aspect of the question at least; and in view of the widespread interest on the subject, which had in some cases taken shape in legislation as much as twenty years before, and had not proved disadvantageous,

---

[1] 9 and 10 Vict., c. 95, s. 83; Starkie on Evidence, p. *139.

the Federal act may have accelerated the movement already begun here.[1]

It was, then, in view of this history and experience of others, and of our own State to some extent, that the legislature approached the consideration of the subject in 1869. There were not wanting patterns from which to frame an act. All of the legislation presented two general distinguishing features. It was open to them, on the one hand, to remove the incompetency of witnesses in certain specific cases, and otherwise remain silent on the subject; or, on the other, to make one sweeping change, and then retracing their steps restore the disqualification in certain excepted cases. They adopted the latter course. On April 15th, 1869, was passed an act[2] entitled "An act allowing parties in interest to be witnesses."

---

[1] 1 Phil. on Ev., Introd. Chap., note to C., H. & E.'s ed., 1859, p. xiii; Act of Congress, July 2d, 1864, 13 Stat. at Large, 351; Rev. Stat., 162, §. 858.

[2] Purdon's Dig., 624, pl. 16; P. L., 30.

CHAPTER III.

THE ACTS OF APRIL 15, 1869, AND APRIL 9, 1870.

SECTION 1 of the Act of April 15th, 1869:

"No interest nor policy of law shall exclude a party or person from being a witness in any civil proceeding; *Provided*, This act shall not alter the law, as now declared and practiced in the courts of this commonwealth, so as to allow husband and wife to testify against each other, nor counsel to testify to the confidential communication of his client; and this act shall not apply to actions by or against executors, administrators or guardians, nor where the assignor of the thing or contract in action may be dead, excepting in issues and inquiries *devisavit vel non* and others, respecting the right of such deceased owner, between parties claiming such right by devolution on the death of such owner."

Within less than one year after, to wit, April 9th, 1870, was passed a supplement, which so evidently was the result of the same thought as that which produced the act of 1869, in merely supplying an omission found to exist in the main act, that it had best be mentioned immediately in connection with it, particularly inasmuch as a reference to it will serve to elucidate the meaning of the former.

The Act of April 9th, 1870, is as follows:[1]

"In all actions or civil proceedings in any of the courts of this commonwealth, brought by or against executors, administrators or guardians, or in actions where the assignor of the thing or contract in action may be dead, no interest or policy of law shall exclude any party to the record from tes-

---

[1] Act of April 9th, 1870, § 1, P. L., 44; Purdon's Dig., 625, pl. 20.

tifying to matters occurring since the death of the person whose estate, through a legal representative, is a party to the record."

We have considered at some length the old law, and have seen how by degrees slight changes were made to remedy the mischiefs which from time to time became most noticeable in it; but there still remained greater mischiefs, which it was now the purpose of legislation to remove. It is important to bear in mind just what the mischief was, and what it was not. It was not the exclusion of certain classes of evidence as the confidential communications of counsel and client, the confidential communications of husband and wife; nor the exclusion of evidence about those things which decency, propriety, and sometimes the public welfare required should not be made the subject of public inquiry; there was no dissatisfaction with the public policy which forbade the disclosure of any one of these things. The mischief was not that certain evidence was excluded, but it was, that certain witnesses were excluded, and held incapable of giving testimony which, given by some one else, was perfectly admissible, and this not because they were always unreliable, but because they might be. It is a rather curious fact that, while the law excluded both parties to a suit, because, as Gilbert said, "it is not to be presumed that a man who complains without cause, or defends without justice, should have honesty enough to confess it,"[1] it did not take into consideration that for the very reason that his testimony was likely to be dishonest, the adversary of such an one would have had every inducement to tell the truth; and as between the two, with the natural tendency of mankind to speak the truth, and the difficulty of maintaining a lie under cross-examination, it might have been supposed that the result would have been the elucidation of truth. This conclusion was arrived at with us before our act was passed. The other, and the moral argument that was sometimes urged, that the

---

[1] *Cf., ante,* p. 20.

parties must be saved from the temptation to perjury, had long since been weakened by the tendency on the part of the State to let all parties take care of themselves in that respect, and practically abandoned by the act of 1865, which threw open the door to perjury of the rankest kind, if it was to be expected at all. But, while on the practical view of the question, the probability of arriving at the truth, opinions had suffered so great a change, it was seen that the view now suggested upon this point was only applicable to those cases in which both parties were on an equality in their opportunity for giving testimony. If only one was heard upon a subject, it might chance to be the very one whose testimony was unreliable, and so, not prepared to give the jury the same opportunity, that they had in all other cases, of judging whether the witness were perjuring himself or not, it was deemed necessary to preserve the equality of the witnesses in some way. It might be practically preserved by excluding a party to a transaction from testifying as to it, unless the opposing party were also present to testify; but this would not exclude him as to other matters in the happening of which the absent party was not present: and, too, it was open to the difficulty that, although the absentee might not have been able to deny the happening of those facts, he might yet be in possession of other facts, the effect of which would be to render the former nugatory. The dilemma was taken by the horns, and no one who was a party or interested was to testify at all when the opposing party, or those in whose shoes he stood, was dead, with one exception in the act of 1869, and a broad exception as to facts occurring since the death of such a person, made by the act of 1870.

As was said, the blow was aimed at the exclusion of witnesses, because they were presumed to be unreliable, not at the exclusion of testimony, nor even of witnesses, where the exclusion was based solely upon the public interest, as in the case of husband and wife testifying against each other, and so out of abundant caution the case of the incompetent testimony of confidential communications of attorney and client, and that of the incompetent witnesses, husband and wife, testifying against each other were protected from any possible operation of the act. We may now examine the act in detail, and see what construction has been placed upon its language.

"No interest nor policy of law shall exclude a party or person from being a witness in any civil proceeding."

Every one whose testimony can be given under the sanction of a legal oath or its equivalent is competent to testify in all civil proceedings except such as fall within the proviso—or subsequent acts.

Most of the cases under this act have arisen upon the interpretation of the proviso, but this clause is open to some question, and it is worth while to make it the subject of discussion. Fortunately, two cases, one quite early and one very recent, have the one in effect, the other, in both language and effect, observed the distinction, and given to the term "policy of the law" its proper interpretation. In *Tioga Co. v. South Creek Township*, 25 Sm., 433 (March, 1874), a proceeding to test the settlement of a pauper, the father and mother of the pauper, who was born shortly after marriage, were both called to prove non-access, and their testimony was subsequently excluded. On writ of error, GORDON, J., in commenting upon the exclusion of their testimony, said: "But the counsel for the appellant insists that the case is within the purview of the act of 1869. The language of that act at first blush might seem to include a case of this kind. . . . . But when we come to consider the fact that '*the interest or policy of law*,' which the legislature had in view in passing that act, was that which, before that time, excluded parties from testifying in their own suits, or where they had an interest in the subject-matter in controversy, it becomes obvious that a case, such as the one under discussion, was not in the legislative mind when that act was passed. It would, therefore, be an unnecessary and violent construction of the statute to make it include a 'policy of law' wholly different from that under contemplation when it was framed.

We, therefore, without hesitation, adopt the view taken of this question by the learned judge of the Court of Quarter Sessions, and agree with him that the Act of 1869 was not intended to abolish a valuable rule of law founded in good morals and public decency." Certainly there can be no doubt that the conclusion reached in this case was correct, but the language of the opinion is much narrower than that of the subsequent case of *Bank* v. *Rhoads*, 8 N., 353 (1879), in which the maker of a note was permitted, in an action by the holder against an indorser, to show that the note had not been regularly negotiated. In the opinion of the court, delivered by STERRETT, J., it is distinctly stated that the ground of exclusion of a party to negotiable paper, under the rule of *Walton* v. *Shelly*, was "policy of law, not interest." Now, if this was the case, and it unquestionably was, then if the legislature had in view in passing the act only the interest or policy of law "which, before that time, excluded parties from testifying in their own suits, or when they had an interest in the subject-matter in controversy," it would be obvious that this case also "was not in the legislative mind when that act was passed," and the witness would still have been incompetent. But the legislature must have had in view more than this, otherwise they would not have especially provided that it should not operate to admit husband and wife to testify against each other, nor the confidential communications of counsel and client, in neither of which cases was interest the ground of exclusion. It is true that the preamble of the act is "An act allowing parties in interest to be witnesses;" but SHARSWOOD, J., had pointed out, in *Yeager* v. *Weaver*, 14 Sm., 425 (1870), that the preamble of the act was not to overrule or control it; he said: " When the title, therefore, speaks of parties in interest, it was cognate with the subject to extend the law to 'persons' not 'parties,' and to those who before had been excluded on the score of policy," and so he had ruled that husband and wife were competent witnesses for each other by virtue of the act, although this was only to be sustained by holding the words policy of the law to mean more than policy based upon interest alone; and the legislature evidently so intended, otherwise it would have been surplusage to add that the act should not operate to permit the testimony of husband and wife against each other. The same view is implied by AGNEW, J., in *Karns* v. *Tanner*, 16 Sm., 297 (1871), who, in referring to this clause said : "This is sweeping language, and was intended to reach every imaginable case. But the legislature knew that there were some exceptions that must be allowed, otherwise the law could not stand, for it would run counter to interests so sacred and a policy so clear, that public sentiment would not tolerate their sacrifice. The proviso therefore, followed, which was evidently the product of two thoughts, one, that there were certain confidential relations to be protected against compulsory disclosure, the other that there were certain cases of inequality where it would be unjust to open a door to one party, that was closed by necessity against the other."

The key to the interpretation of the act on this point is found by STERRETT, J., in *Bank* v. *Rhoads*. He there says: "The design of the act was to make competent all who are not within the scope of the proviso; but it was not intended to convert into *competent* testimony that which was before *incompetent*. The act operates not on evidence, but on persons, by removing the disqualification to testify which previously attached to them on account of the policy of law or personal interest in the subject-matter of the controversy. If not excluded by the proviso to the act, the witness is competent to testify to whatever might have been proved before by any competent and disinterested witness." This does not conflict with the ruling in *Tioga* v. *South Creek Township*, for there it was the *fact* which the law forbid being disclosed, and the testimony of that fact was inadmissible, not the witness by whom alone it could have been proven.

The result of this argument, if it has been proven, is to show that the act of 1869 has removed all incompetency of witnesses arising from a presumption of want of integrity, or the mere policy of the law, and amongst these, of course, is that arising from infamy. It is true that in *Schuylkill Co.* v. *Coply*, 17 Sm., 386 (1871), this view was not suggested, and the witness was held competent on other grounds; but it does not follow that had it been called to the attention of the court it would not have prevailed. Incompetency on this ground had long since been removed absolutely in England and in many of the States, and, in others, was only permitted to go to the credibility of the witness;[1] and, with the sweeping language used in the act of 1869, it seems probable that a sweeping change in the law upon the subject was intended to be made. It is true that the proviso, which is evidently intended to cover all cases covered by the enabling clause, may be said to be unnecessary in such a case as infamy; but that argument applies no more to the case of infamy than to that of husband and wife; in fact, it is impossible, within the compass of any reasonable act, to make its provisions absolutely consistent, as the frequent subsequent amendments have only too plainly shown. It may be said, however, if the act goes so far as this, why not extend its operation to the case of persons incompetent by reason of mental or moral defect? The answer is, that there is no intimation in the act that the method of obtaining the testimony of witnesses is to be abandoned, and so long as the legal oath, or its equivalent, is the only recognized sanction of any witness's testimony, whatever will prevent him from qualifying himself by it must remain as a bar to his becoming a witness; but when he is, himself, free from such an impediment, the law has removed every other objection.

---

[1] Connecticut, Michigan, Massachusetts, Iowa, etc. 1 Phillips on Evidence, Int. Chap. and C. H. & E.'s, note.

CHAPTER IV.

THE FIRST CLAUSE OF THE PROVISO TO THE ACT OF APRIL 15TH, 1869.

"This act shall not alter the law as now declared and practiced in the courts of this Commonwealth, so as to allow husband and wife to testify against each other."

The law, as then "declared and practiced," excluded both husband and wife from testifying at the call of either side in any case in which one of them was a party, or interested.[1] The rule was founded, partly upon interest, and partly upon public policy alone; but it was not difficult of application, for wherever one was incompetent from interest, the other was incompetent to testify at the call of either party to the suit. This incompetency of husband and wife to testify, for or against the interest of the other, was, of course, quite different from the incompetency of evidence of confidential communications made by one to the other; in the one case, the witnesses were incompetent, in the other, the evidence.

Under the act, both husband and wife are competent witnesses for each other.

It was said in one of the lower courts, less than a year after the passage of the act, that it authorized husband and wife to testify neither for nor against each other, *Bast* v. *Anspach*, 2 Leg. Gaz., 6 (C. P., December, 1869), but, as we have already seen, in the next year the Supreme Court decided that they were competent *for* each other, *Yeager* v. *Weaver*, 14 Sm., 425 (Mch., 1870).[2] It was urged as one ground to show that the act could have no such meaning,

---

[1] Pringle *v.* Pringle, 9 Sm., 281.
[2] *Ante*, p. 89. See, also, Cawley *v.* Wilson, 7 Ph., 676 (C. P.).

that, if it were permitted, the result of a cross-examination might be to require one of them to testify against the other, and, since the provision was inserted to exclude this very case, it could never have been contemplated that they should be placed in such a position; this argument was characterized as ingenious but not sound, for the party calling a witness must invariably take the consequences of his testimony. There was no more reason for saying that this result should operate to exclude under the act of 1869 than that the similar result of the act of 1865 should cause it to be nugatory. The legislature must be presumed to have had this result in contemplation when they passed the act. The same argument was repeated in *Ballentine* v. *White*, 27 Sm., 20 (Nov., 1874), where the wife of the plaintiff was called to testify on his behalf, and SHARSWOOD, J., repeated, in effect, what he had said in *Yeager* v. *Weaver*, upon the same point: "The proviso only excepts the case of husband and wife testifying against each other. . . . . When admitted, as by the act she must be, her husband must take all the risks of what her evidence will be, whether upon examination in chief or cross-examination."[1] It is, then, clear enough that when the action is not one within the terms of the proviso, the act has made husband and wife competent for each other, but left them incompetent against each other.

(1.) *The Effect to be Given to the Testimony of Husband or Wife for the Other.*—It seems to have been supposed that the case of *Sower* v. *Weaver*, 28 Sm., 443 (1 W. N. C., 499, May, 1875), held the testimony of both husband and wife in support of the husband's title to land to be equivalent to that of but one witness.[2] This inference is hardly deducible from the case, however, and is in conflict with the spirit of other decisions. The case was an action of ejectment, in which a parol gift of the land was set up as an equitable defence; the testimony of the defendant as to the gift

---

[1] The same rule was recognized in Craig v. Brendel, 19 Sm., 153; which, however, is discussed elsewhere. *Cf.* p. 116.

[2] See the syllabus.

was positive, but that of the wife did not come up to the requirements. It is true that SHARSWOOD, J., said: "Admitting Weaver and his wife to amount together to one sufficient witness, where is the remaining witness, or that which is equivalent thereto?" But it is evident from the report that the testimony of the wife was not regarded as in character equal to the necessity of the case. To hold that had it been, it would nevertheless not be equal in *competency* to that of any other witness, would have been contrary to all the decisions as to the effect to be given to the testimony of those witnesses rendered competent by statute.[1]

(2.) *What is Interest against Husband or Wife.*—It has been said that the law as it stood at the time of the passage of the act excluded both husband and wife from testifying for either side in a cause in which the other had an interest. It was not necessary that the one should be a party to the cause, it was only necessary that a legal interest in either side should exist.[2] Where the incompetency was removed so far as to permit either to testify in favor of the other, and only to exclude them from testifying against each other, the rule for determining the competency under the act ought to be very simple. It would require but to ascertain whether either husband or wife has a legal interest in the event of the suit (and this may be either in the issue or in the record as an instrument of evidence), and if so, then the other is incompetent to testify for the side adverse to that interest. In the first case which came up for consideration, where the question was really directly raised, a decision was made, which it seems more than probable would, on review, be overruled; it was the case of *Musser* v. *Gardner*, 16 Sm., 242 (January, 1871). One Gardner, who had possession of some personal property of his wife's, sold it without any authority from her and absconded: she was in fact a *feme sole* trader, but she brought replevin against the purchaser

---

[1] *Postea*, p. 157.

[2] Greenleaf on Evidence, §§ 335 and 342, n. 4; *Gross* v. *Reddig*, 9 Wr., 406; *Pringle* v. *Pringle*, 9 Sm., 281, *supra*, p. 92.

in the name of Gardner and herself in her right. The issue was joined on defendant's plea of "property;" on the trial the husband's name was stricken from the record. The issue, of course, was whether the husband had given any title to the defendant by the sale, he was therefore so far interested in the warranty of title, that, had the suit been by a stranger, his interest would before the act have rendered him incompetent for the defendant.[1] The rule suggested above, however, was not applied by the court, THOMPSON, C. J., who delivered the opinion, saying: "The husband was no party, and that he might possibly be called on at some time or other to answer on an implied warranty of title to the property he had sold and now claimed by the wife, was too remote and contingent to bring her within the prohibition of the statute from testifying against her husband." But this was not such a remote interest but that it would have excluded him from testifying on the other side, had he been called. In the two following cases the old rule was strictly adhered to.

The first of these was *Rowley* v. *McHugh*, 16 Sm., 269 (Jan., 1871), which was ejectment by Rowley and wife, in her right, against McHugh *et al.* The title was in Rowley's wife, but it had been sold by the sheriff as the property of the husband, and defendants claimed under the sheriff's vendee. The plaintiffs offered the wife as a witness, but she was excluded, and the verdict being for defendants, the plaintiffs took a writ of error. WILLIAMS, J., said: "Here the wife was not called to testify against the husband, but in her own behalf. The ejectment was in her own right, and the husband was only a nominal party to the proceeding. If he had any interest in the event of his wife's recovery, it was contingent and on the side of the wife. The argument that the wife was called to testify against the husband, because the defendants claimed title under the sheriff's sale of the land as the husband's property, has no foundation for its support. The husband did not warrant,

---

[1] Whitney *v.* Shippen, 2 W. N. C., 470 (March, 1876).

and he is in nowise responsible for the validity of the defendant's title, nor has he any interest in maintaining it. It is clear then that the wife was not called to testify against her husband in any sense, but in her own favor, and in behalf of her husband so far as it respects his contingent interest in the event of her recovery." The judgment was therefore reversed.

McGeary's Appeal, 22 Sm., 365 (Jan., 1873), was an appeal from a decree confirming an auditor's report distributing the proceeds of a sale under a *levari facias sur* mortgage of Groves and wife. The contest was between a judgment creditor of the husband and the Pittsburg Insurance Company, a mortgagee of the husband and wife, whose mortgage was, however, inefficiently acknowledged by the wife, on one side, and a subsequent mortgagee of the husband and wife on the other. The title was in the wife, but it was claimed that the property really was the husband's. At the call of the insurance company the wife was permitted to testify as to facts, which showed, that as matter of law, the property belonged to him, of which facts the subsequent mortgagee had notice, and the fund being too small to meet all of the claims, the subsequent mortgagee was excluded from participation in it. On appeal the decree of the court below was affirmed, READ, C. J., saying: "She also was a competent witness, as she was not testifying against her husband, but only to the truth as regarded herself."

The principal question for consideration then is, how are we to determine what is testimony of a husband or wife against the other? Notwithstanding the case of *Musser* v. *Gardner*, which certainly points to an interest in the *issue* as the only one sufficient to exclude, the rule suggested above can be regarded as the only safe one, viz.: that any interest in the suit which before the act would have rendered husband or wife incompetent for one side is sufficient to render the other incompetent for the other side.

(3.) *Testimony of Husband or Wife for or against the Estate of the other.*—It is not alone when the husband or wife is personally interested in the result of a suit that the other is excluded as a witness against that interest, the same protection extends to their estates in the hands of those who take them upon their deaths. *McBride's Appeal*, 22 Sm., 480 (Jan., 1872). It is immaterial what the form of action is: if the result of the testimony is to decrease the estate of the decedent or prevent from going into it that which would otherwise increase its value, the survivor is incompetent. *Boyle* v. *Haughey*, 5 Leg. G., 406 (C. P., Dec., 1873). Still less competent is evidence of the declarations made by one against the other, even though the same evidence from another might be competent. *Derrickson* v. *Wilbur*, 7 Ph., 169 (Jan., 1870).

The question arose in *Greenawalt* v. *McEnelly*, 4 N., 352 (November, 1877), whether in a contest between the alleged heirs of her husband, the wife was competent to testify as to the fact of her marriage in order to prove the legitimacy of the daughter. She was held competent, PAXSON, J., who delivered the opinion of the court, saying: "She was not called to testify against her husband, nor to any fact the knowledge of which was acquired by reason of her confidential relations with him, but as to matters acquired within her own knowledge." The same principle had been enunciated in *Hopple's Est.*, 3 W. N. C., 79 (O. C., October, 1876), in an appeal from the Register refusing an issue *devisavit vel non*. It is, therefore, beyond doubt that in contests between persons claiming the estate of her deceased husband as heirs or beneficiaries, the wife is not rendered incompetent by the reservation in the act.

(4.) *Confidential Communications.*—The theory upon which this act is viewed throughout being that of its effect upon persons and not evidence, it is only necessary in passing to remark that the inadmissibility of confidential communications between husband and wife, of course, remains as before; this has been recognized, though not specifically decided, in *Conrad* v. *Conrad*, 4 W. N. C., 2 (March, 1877), and *Greenawalt* v. *McEnelly*, 4 N., 352 (November, 1877).

"**Counsel to Testify to the Confidential Communications of their Clients.**"—The observation just made with reference to the confidential communications between husband and wife is equally applicable to the case of counsel and client. The act is too explicit to permit of any argument being made upon this point, which is one belonging to the competency of evidence, rather than that of witnesses. It is enough to say that the rule excluding such evidence has been distinctly affirmed to be in force since the passage of the act, by the lower courts at least. *Parce* v. *Stetson,* 2 W. N. C., 110 (C. P., October, 1875); *Bennett's Estate,* 8 W. N. C., 287 (O. C., February, 1880).

CHAPTER V.

THE SECOND CLAUSE OF THE PROVISO.

"**And this act shall not apply to actions by or against executors, administrators, or guardians, nor where the assignor of the thing or contract in action may be dead, excepting in issues and inquiries** *devisavit vel non* **and others, respecting the right of such deceased owner, between parties claiming such right by devolution on the death of such owner.**"

We have seen how far the great object of the act, the removal of all the disabilities of witnesses save one, that of husband and wife to testify against each other, has been recognized and carried out; it remains to consider how far the correlative object, the exclusion from its effect of those cases in which it was thought that it could not safely be permitted to operate, has been sustained by the language of the proviso and its interpretation.

Before proceeding to a discussion of this proviso as a whole, and in its separate clauses, it is necessary to understand exactly to what kind of cases it applies, whether the word "actions" means only common-law actions, technically so called, or whether it applies to all forms of judicial proceedings, as well to those in equity and in the Orphans' Court as to those at common law. Happily, whatever doubt might have existed upon this point can be definitely set at rest by a single case, while all of the cases hereafter to be cited have silently acquiesced in its decision.

Meaning of "**Actions.**"—It was urged in *McBride's Appeal*, 22 Sm., 480 (Jan., 1872), that this portion of the proviso did not apply to proceedings in the Orphans' Court in the settlement of estates, that the change of phraseology from "civil proceedings" in the enacting clause to "action" in the proviso was an intentional restriction of the proviso to actions at common law as distinguished from other civil proceedings, but said WILLIAMS, J.: "That the term 'actions,' as used in the proviso, was intended to embrace all civil proceedings, of whatever kind, is evident from the supplement of the 9th of April, 1870, which declares that 'in all actions or civil proceedings in any of the courts of this Commonwealth brought by or against executors, administrators or guardians, or in actions where the assignor of the thing, or contract in action, may be dead, no interest or policy of law shall exclude any party to the record from testifying to matters occurring since the death of the person whose estate, through a legal representative, is a party to the record.' The purpose of the supplement is obvious: It was intended to permit a party, who would otherwise have been excluded by the proviso in the original act, to testify to matters occurring since the death of the person whose estate, through a legal representative, is a party to the record. And it shows that, in the legislative understanding, the word 'actions,' as used in the proviso, was intended to embrace civil proceedings, whatever their form, as well as actions technically so called. If this was not the intention and understanding of the law-making power, why were issues and inquiries *devisavit vel non*, etc., excepted from the 'actions' to which it was declared that the act should not apply? Besides, a suit or action, according to its legal definition, is the lawful demand of one's right in a court of justice: *jus prosequendi in judicio quod alicui debitur*: 3 Black. Com., 116. This definition is broad enough to include the proceeding in this case."

The construction thus placed upon the language of the proviso, it will be seen throughout the discussion of it, has always been followed, indeed, had already been recognized in the Supreme Court,[1] and no subsequent attempt to limit its operation to any particular form of proceeding seems ever to have been made.

It being understood, therefore, that the proviso applies to all forms of judicial proceedings, it will be noticed in the first place

---

[1] Breneman's Est., 15 Sm., 298 (1870).

that it does not refer to particular persons as to whom the enabling clause of the act shall be nugatory, nor to particular testimony given by any person; it simply says, that in certain *cases* the act shall not apply.[1] It is important to keep this in mind, because, as we shall see, some confusion has occurred from endeavoring to remedy the defects of the act by its interpretation, which has resulted in occasionally giving it a meaning, which, however reasonable and desirable for it to have, is not warranted by the language. There is this qualification to be made, however, that the act of 1870, which followed so soon upon it, and which, so far as nearly all of the cases go, may really be read into it, does limit the operation of the proviso to certain testimony, and it may always be remembered in considering any case of incompetency under the proviso, that as regards parties to the suit, it limits the operation of the enabling clause only so far as their testimony relates to facts existing prior to the death of the person whose estate through a legal representative is a party to the record. There are but two really difficult points to settle in considering this portion of the act: first, who is an assignor; and, second, whether a person excluded by the proviso is excluded absolutely from testifying as to any facts existing prior to the death of the person whose death excludes, or whether it is only as to transactions with the dead man. The consideration of the questions arising in actions by or against executors, administrators, or guardians is comparatively without difficulty, and this we may proceed with at once, remembering, however, that the question of the extent to which the exclusion goes yet remains to be considered.

Actions by or against Executors or Administrators.—These may be divided into: (1), The settlement of estates in the Orphans' Court; and (2), suits either at common law or in equity.

In the settlement of estates in the Orphans' Court, and in all actions either at common law or in equity by or against executors,

---

[1] TRUNKEY, J., in Hess *v.* Gourley, 7 W. N. C., 158.

administrators, or guardians, all[1] *parties and interested persons, except executors, administrators, trustees, or other persons acting in a fiduciary or representative character, and not having any interest in the subject-matter of controversy, are incompetent to testify as to any facts*[2] *existing prior to the death of the person whose estate through a legal representative is a party to the record.*

(1.) *The Settlement of Estates in the Orphans' Court.*—The first reported case upon the construction of any part of this, the first section of the act, arose in the Orphans' Court of Philadelphia County, before ALLISON, P. J., who held an executor incompetent to prove his own claim against his testator's estate: *Fayle's Estate*, 3 Brews., 564 (O. C., October, 1869). The same construction was recognized in *Breneman's Estate*, 15 Sm., 298 (May, 1870), in which an administrator had been permitted to substantiate his own claim against the estate, and while the Supreme Court did not reverse because there was other sufficient testimony to that effect, it was stated as matter of law that he was incompetent. The same opinion was expressed in *McBride's Appeal, supra.*[3] It was, however, specifically decided in *Gyger's Appeal*, 24 Sm., 42 (July, 1873), where a distributee was held incompetent to testify as to transactions in the lifetime of the decedent in order to reduce the amount of a claim by the estate against himself.[4]

It has been said, that in the settlement of decedents' estates, even though no objection has been raised, it is the duty of the auditor to exclude incompetent witnesses, unless all parties interested agree in writing, so that it may appear upon the report. *Per* FINLETTER, J., *Young's Estate*, 9 Ph., 348 (O. C., Feb., 1874).

---

[1] *Postea*, p. 124. [2] *Postea*, p. 115.
[3] 22 Sm., 480 (Jan., 1872).
[4] Murray's Est., 2 Pears., 473 (C. P., Oct., 1870); Est. John Blantz, 4 L. Bar. (O. C., Nov., 1872); Young's Est., 9 Ph., 348 (C. P., Feb., 1874); Bierly's Appeal, 3 W. N. C., 210 (May, 1876). *In re* Saml. Knubb, 1 Leg. Ch. R., 337.

But while a claimant is incompetent to prove his own claim on his own behalf, it seems that the act of March 29th, 1832, § 56, is still in force, and the auditor or court may require the testimony of an interested party to be given: *Iturbide's Estate*, 1 W. N. C., 316 (O. C., March, 1875); *Hyneman's Estate*, 2 W. N. C., 571 (O. C., May, 1876);[1] and as will appear hereafter, the second section of the Act of April 15th, 1869, can be used for the same purpose at the instance of the adverse party.[2]

It seems that the mere fact of a party to a suit being an executor is not sufficient to exclude the adverse party if the title under which the executor prosecutes or defends was acquired subsequently to the death of his testator, as where he has brought ejectment for land purchased by him as executor and trustee: *Chase* v. *Irvin's Executors*, 6 N., 286 (7 W. N. C., 529, June, 1878); here the argument from inequality has no place, for the decedent had no knowledge of the transaction, and his testimony, even if obtainable, could avail nothing by way of contradiction of his executor's opponent, for the transaction was wholly with the living executor. Suppose, however, in such a case, the original executor to be dead, and an administrator *d. b. n.* to be substituted, does the death of the executor preclude anybody from testifying? It clearly does not as being a case within this clause, but whether or not it does so upon the ground of the original executor being an "assignor," depends upon our understanding of that term as hereafter defined.[3]

(2.) *Suits at Common Law or in Equity.*

(*a.*) *When the witness is a party to the record.*—This is so plain a case under the proviso to the act that the cases have rather accepted as a fact than actually decided the incompetency of a party, except where some other facts in the case raised new questions. The incompetency of a defendant, on the one hand, and a plaintiff on the other, was recognized in *Allum's Executors* v. *Carroll's Administrators et al.*, 17 Sm., 68 (January, 1871), and *Eilbert*

---

[1] S. C., 11 Ph., 135.   [2] *Postea*, p. 138.   [3] *Cf.* p. 123.

v. *Finkbeiner*, 18 Sm., 243 (March, 1871), and specifically decided in two subsequent cases. The defendants were held incompetent in *Hoopes* v. *Beale*, 9 N. 82 (May, 1879), where debt on a bond was brought by Hoopes, to use of Hoopes, administrator of Bailey, against Beale, Wells *et al.*, members of Williamson Lodge, No. 309, and in *Hepburn*, to the use of *Claxton's Administrators* v. *Gamble*, 9 N., 439 (June, 1879). It will be observed that in the last two cases the administrators were the use plaintiffs, and the defendants were held incompetent as to any facts prior to the death of their intestates; if the executor or administrator were that of the plaintiff to use, then it might even be said that still the act literally applied, for it would be the case of an action by an executor or administrator, but in that event the other clause of the proviso would exclude the defendant, because the use plaintiff could not be an executor or administrator unless the assignor of the thing or contract in action were dead.

(*b.*) *When the Witness Offered is not a Party to the Record.*— Four cases illustrating the application of the proviso on this point are to be cited. The rule to apply for the purpose of ascertaining the applicability of the proviso is simple enough. Is the case one by or against an executor or administrator? Would the interest of the witness have rendered him incompetent had the act never been passed? If both these conditions exist then he is certainly incompetent as to all facts prior to the death of the person whose estate, through a legal representative, is a party to the record.[1]

In *Watts* v. *Leidig*, 29 Leg. Int., 293 (May, 1872), one McGowan had given a bond to Frederick Watts, part of which was paid, and an action was brought by Watts against Leidig, McGowan's administrator, to recover the balance. On the trial it was proven that the bond had been given as part of the purchase-money of land sold by William M. Watts to McGowan, and that

---

[1] Until the act of May 11th, 1881 (*q. v.*, p. 155), an interested person not a party was incompetent as to facts, both before and after the death. *Vide*, p. 115.

the bond had been given to Frederick Watts by agreement with William M. Watts in settlement of an account between them. It was admitted that the title to the land had partially failed. In rebuttal the plaintiff offered to prove by William M. Watts that "it was understood that the title was to be at the risk of McGowan," and other facts connected with the original transaction. He was held incompetent. The ground taken by the lower court, and affirmed on writ of error without an opinion, was because he was "a party to the contract," and "so far as he and McGowan were concerned, and just so far as plaintiff attempts to support the consideration of the bond in suit by the contract (the sale of the land) between him and McGowan, he is not a competent witness." It would seem that this was a very unnecessary process of reasoning by which to exclude him; it proceeded, however, upon the theory, which was for some time held, that an interested witness was competent for some purposes, but not for others, in cases within the proviso. It has been attempted elsewhere[1] to show that this has been rightly repudiated, and in view of the present theory of interpretation it would be enough to say that this was an action against an administrator, and the witness was interested, he was therefore incompetent to testify as to any fact prior to the death of the deceased person whose estate was a party to the record. (The question of the release given in this case is also discussed hereafter.)[2]

Hogeboom's Executor v. *Gibbs, Sterrett & Co.*, 7 N., 235 (7 W. N. C., 399, January, 1879), was an action of assumpsit by Gibbs, Sterrett & Co. against J. C. Hogeboom, executor of Henry Hogeboom, deceased, defendant, who was impleaded with his alleged partners, Philip and Sherman; issue was joined with the executor alone, who pleaded that his testator was not a partner. It was held that the deposition of Philip was inadmissible to prove the partnership. He was inadmissible before the act, and was not rendered competent by the act. *Whitney* v. *Shippen*, 2 W. N. C., 470 (March,

---

[1] *Postea*, p. 115. [2] *Postea*, p. 162.

1876), was debt on a lease, brought by Shippen *et al.*, executors of Gray, against Whitney, for the rent of a brewery under a lease to Martin, containing an agreement that no alteration nor improvements should be removed. Martin had assigned the lease to Whitney, who offered Martin as a witness to prove an express parol agreement with Gray that he might sell or remove a boiler erected by him, which plaintiff had retained, and for which Whitney claimed set-off, and that he sold it to Whitney with Gray's knowledge. It was held that he was properly excluded, because being vendor he had impliedly warranted the title, and was therefore interested, before the act of 1869, which did not relieve him.[1] The same point was ruled in a subsequent case between the same parties in *Whitney* v. *Shippen*, 8 N., 22 (February, 1879), which was an action of covenant, when Martin was again called to give the same testimony.

Actions by or against Guardians.—No portion of the act has received so little comment as this, probably because so few cases ever arise in which a guardian is one of the litigant parties. The case of a guardian was evidently put in the same position as that of an executor, because in most cases a guardian of personalty, like an executor, represents only the estate of a deceased person, which he holds in trust for his ward; but in this position there is but little opportunity for litigation in his name, for whatever claims or liabilities have formed part of the decedent's estate are apt to have been settled by the executor or administrator before the estate was transferred to him; and in the case of a guardian of either real or personal estate the case would, of course, come within the definition of one in which the "assignor" is dead. The most frequent case in which testimony for or against a guardian can be necessary is in the settlement of his own account, and on this alone is there any authority, a single case, and that in a lower court: *Rutherford's Estate*, 2 W. N. C., 493 (O. C., March, 1876), in which a

---

[1] This was recognized in Agnew v. Whitney, 2 W. N. C.; 474 (C. P.).

ward was held competent to impeach the testimony of his guardian as to items contained in the account, because it was said he was rendered so by the act of April 9th, 1870.[1] Indeed, since the passage of that act it would seem that in no case will incompetency exist in actions by or against guardians, except those covered by the deceased assignor clause.

"**Where the Assignor of the Thing or Contract in Action may be Dead.**" (1)—*An " assignor" is one whose beneficial interest in or liability arising out of the thing or contract in action has fallen upon one of the parties to the action by virtue of either a voluntary act or by operation of law.*

The terms used are very broad, and it remained for the courts to determine what was meant by a thing or contract in action, and who is an assignor within the meaning of this expression. The expressions "thing in action," "contract in action," remind us at once of the old rule excluding under all circumstances the assignor of a chose in action, or one of the parties to a contract, from testifying for his assignee in a suit to recover the one or enforce the other. But most important of all is the determination of the meaning of the term "assignor," for the expression must be construed as a whole in order to determine whose death it is which closes the mouth of a party or an interested person. For the purpose of determining both of these points, we will consider at some length all of those cases which have arisen where it can be said that any new phase of the situation has presented itself for settlement, keeping in view the fact that the term assignor may be defined either with reference to the character of the assignment or the position of the assignor in the line of title.

One of the very first cases under the act throws great light on both points; it was the case of (a) *Karns* v. *Tanner*, 16 Sm., 297 (Jan. 1871), already referred to; the facts were these: Parker leased to Tanner; subsequently Parker, alleging a forfeiture by Tanner, leased again to Karns & Co. Tanner brought ejectment

---

[1] *Postea*, p. 131.

against Parker and Karns & Co., but died. His interest in the land was sold at sheriff's sale and bought by Frances E. Tanner, who was substituted as plaintiff in the case. On the trial the question was of course the forfeiture by Tanner. Parker, the lessor, was held incompetent to testify on behalf of the defendants. It is to be noticed, as was said by the court, "In a precise sense then James P. Tanner, the deceased lessee of the premises, is not the assignor of Frances E. Tanner, for he was dead before his title passed; and it passed by a sheriff's sale by act of the law. He therefore did not assign. Again, the thing in action is the right to the possession of the premises leased, this being an action of ejectment, and the contract under which this right arises is the lease from Parker to Tanner. In that lease Parker is the lessor, and may be said to be the assignor to Tanner of the thing in action, and Parker is alive. As assignor to Tanner, he seems literally not to be within the prohibition of the proviso. But is this the true meaning of the proviso? We think not." The state of the law from Steele *v.* Phœnix Ins. Co., until Cambria Iron Co. *v.* Tombs, is then briefly passed in review, and the necessity for the change which brought about the act, and after referring to the thoughts contained in the proviso, the opinion proceeds: "Where one of two parties to a transaction is dead, the survivor and the party representing the deceased party, stand on an unequal footing as to a knowledge of the transaction occurring in the lifetime of the deceased. The enacting clause had opened the lips of all parties, but when death came it closed the lips of one, and even-handed justice required the mouths of both to be sealed. In regard to one class we easily comprehend that a survivor ought not to be permitted to testify against the executor or administrator of his adversary, but, as to the other class in the same clause, we do not so readily perceive what *assignor* it is, who being dead the proviso closes the mouth of the survivor. Evidently it is the true purpose of the proviso to close the mouth of him who is adversary to the deceased assignor. Here the current of former decisions tends to elucidate the meaning of the legislature. If, therefore, the holder of a note, bond or other contract should assign his interest to another, he was held to be incompetent to support the claim by his testimony against the opposite party in the instrument or contract. Hence, although he had been stripped of all apparent interest by his assignment, or by the operation of the bankrupt law, yet he could not testify against the adverse party. One of the reasons given by Woodward, J., in Graves v. Griffin, *supra*, is that whilst one of the parties to a contract in litigation is denied the privilege of testifying, the policy of the law is to close the mouth of the other, and this whether it relates to a claim of a plaintiff, or a set-off of a defendant. The true spirit of the proviso then seems to be that when a party to a thing or contract in action is dead, and his rights have passed, either by his own act or by that of the law, to another who represents his interest in the subject of controversy, the surviving party to that subject shall not testify to matters occurring in the lifetime of the adverse party, whose lips are now closed.

"This intent is gathered also from the coupling of the provision for the assignor who is dead, with the provision for the case of an executor or administrator, evidencing that the legislature looked upon both cases as precisely alike. Another clue to the meaning is found in the exception to the proviso found in the last clause; excepting all 'issues and inquiries *devisavit vel non* and others respecting the right of such deceased owner between parties claiming such right by devolution on the death of such owner.' Thus parties claiming under the same decedent, by the mere operation of the law devolving the estate upon them, as by descent or succession, are exempted from the prohibition of the proviso, in contrast to those who stand in adversary relation by reason of a subject of contract, one side of which has come from one of the original parties to the disputed subject. The true intent of the legislature is further developed by the act of 9th of April, 1870, declaring 'that in all actions or civil proceedings in any of the courts of this Commonwealth, brought by or against executors, administrators or guardians, or in actions where the assignor of the thing or contract in action may be dead, no interest or policy of law shall exclude any party to the record from testifying to matters occurring since the death of the person whose estate, through a legal representative, is a party to the record.' Here the terms 'since the death of the person whose estate *through a legal representative* is a party to the record,' are striking, for both classes are linked together in the same clause, and the terms, 'through a legal representative,' applied to the case of a deceased assignor as well as to the case of an executor or administrator, evincing the intention of the legislature not to confine the term assignor to one who has by his own act merely transferred his title, but rather to treat the correlative term assignee just as the term assignees is oftentimes used, in a broad sense, including any one taking title by a sheriff's sale, an Orphans' Court sale, or even a devise under a will."

(*b*.) *Hanna* v. *Wray*, 27 Sm., 27 (1 W. N. C., 65, November, 1874), was an action of assumpsit by Robert Wray, against I. B. McVay, C. B. McVay, and James P. Hanna, partners. On the plaintiff's motion the name of C. B. McVay was stricken from the record. After the cause was at issue I. B. McVay died. The jury were sworn as to Hanna only as surviving partner. At the trial Wray was permitted to testify as to transactions between himself and I. B. McVay, but on writ of error it was *held*, that this was error, and it was left as *quære* whether his testimony as to transactions between himself and Hanna alone would be competent.

(*c*.) *Gardner* v. *McLallen*, 29 Sm., 398 (November, 1875), was an action of ejectment by Olivia Gardner and her husband, in her right, against Catharine McLallen, widow of Henry McLallen; the plaintiff claimed as heir of Henry McLallen, the defendant, as survivor of her husband, with whom she claimed to have held the land by entireties. The defendant was held incompetent to testify as to the circumstances of the contract for the land, and the payment by her of most of the purchase-money, because of the death of Henry McLallen, through whom the plaintiff derived title.

(*d.*) *Gavit* v. *Supplee*, 2 W. N. C., 561 (March, 1876), was an action of assumpsit by Supplee, surviving partner of Stanhope & Supplee, against Gavit. Supplee testified as to the making of the contract and the delivery of the goods, but admitted that the contract was not made in his presence. The defendant was *held* incompetent to show what was the verbal contract with Stanhope, the deceased member of the firm. (A point was made in the Supreme Court, for the first time, that the defendant was at least competent to refute the plaintiff's testimony.)

(*e.*) *Stanbridge* v. *Catanach*, 2 N., 368 (4 W. N. C., 176, February, 1877), was assumpsit by Adam Catanach, surviving partner of Catanach & Son, against G. O. Stanbridge, surviving partner of Stanbridge Bros., to recover the balance of a bill for work and labor done. The defence was that the order had been given by defendant's father, who had no connection with the firm. Plaintiffs proved by their foreman a contract made with deceased member of defendant's firm, by the deceased member of the plaintiff's firm. G. O. Stanbridge was offered to prove "that the defendant's firm never ordered the case, which is the subject of the suit, and that the same was not, in fact, delivered to them," but under the authority of Hanna *v.* Wray he was *held* incompetent.[1]

(*f.*) In *Arthurs* v. *King et al.*, 3 Nor., 525 (October, 1877), ejectment was brought by Arthurs against King and Fuller for a tract of land claimed by Arthurs under a deed from the executor of one Zimmerman. The defendants claimed title as tenants under a deed alleged to have been made by Zimmerman himself to one Bascom, through a purchase from Boyer, to whom Zimmerman had by parol agreed to sell, and who before the deed was made out had resold to Bascom, to whom the conveyance was made directly. Boyer and Bascom were both alive, and Boyer was interested in

---

[1] Runkel *v.* Phillips, 9 Ph., 619 (C. P.), *contra*, was decided in June, 1872.

sustaining the title derived through him in order to secure the unpaid purchase-money. On the trial the depositions of Boyer and Bascom in relation to the alleged purchase from Zimmerman were admitted in evidence, but on writ of error it was *held* that the death of Zimmerman, to whose rights, as against the defendants, the plaintiff had succeeded, excluded both of them from testifying as to any facts alleged to have taken place in his lifetime, which tended to prove the issue.

(*g.*) *Brady* v. *Reed*, 6 N., 111 (May, 1878), was assumpsit by Brady against Reed, Henderson, and Hiester, trading as Reed, Henderson & Co. Before the trial Hiester died, and under the act of March 22d, 1861, his executors were substituted. Brady offered himself as a witness as to transactions, none of which were with Hiester. *Held* that he was incompetent, because the rights and liabilities of Hiester had descended to the surviving partners as co-defendants, and he was thus their assignor, and also because it was an action against executors.[1]

(*h.*) In *Chase* v. *Irvin's Executors* 6 N., 286 (June, 1878, 7 W. N. C., 529), ejectment was brought by Irvin's executors against Chase, for land sold as the property of W. A. Dunlap under a judgment obtained by Irvin against him, and to which they had taken title as trustees. Chase was offered as a witness to prove certain admissions of Isaac Dunlap, under whom the plaintiffs claimed title, but he was rejected, and on writ of error *held* incompetent.

(*i.*) *Hess* v. *Gourley*, 8 N. 195 (7 W. N. C., 157, March, 1879), was an action of ejectment by John and Ann Gourley, in her right, against Peter and Maria Hess *et al.* The plaintiff claimed the land as an heir of one Barber, the defendants claimed under a de-

---

[1] Noble *v.* Mortimer, 4 W. N. C., 300 (C. P., July, 1877), was a case in which a *silent partner* had died, but YERKES, J., said that they were governed by Hanna *v.* Wray, and Stanbridge *v.* Catanach, from which they could not distinguish this case.

For the amendment to the law as it respects partners, see *postea*, p. 154.

vise from Barber's wife, with whose money they alleged that the property had been purchased. The defendants offered the deposition of Peter and Maria Hess to prove these facts, all which took place in Barber's lifetime, but they were excluded. On writ of error taken by the defendants, the judgment was affirmed, TRUNKEY, J., saying: "In the statutory sense the assignor of the thing or contract is he whose right therein or thereunder, at or before the time of his decease, passed by his own act, or by law, to a party in the action. The defendant, Maria Hess, claims title under the will of Ann Barber. Alexander Barber died intestate, and the plaintiff, one of his four nephews and nieces, avers that he was owner of the land in controversy, which passed to them by operation of law. The assignor of the thing in action is dead, his right has passed to the plaintiff, and the statutory rule of evidence does not apply, except to matters which have occurred since his decease."

(*k*.) *Ewing* v. *Ewing*, 9 W. N. C., 489 (January, 1881), Ejectment by Ann L. Ewing, against John K. Ewing. Plaintiff claimed under a devise from her husband, to whom a deed had been made, August 12th, 1847. The defendant claimed as having held adverse possession since 1848, and under objection he was permitted to testify as to facts occurring in his father's lifetime, but not as to any transaction with him. On writ of error, however, it was *held*, that it was error to have admitted him at all.

First, *as to what is meant by "the thing or contract in action."*— Upon examining the cases cited, we find that in six (*a, c, f, h, i, k*) out of the ten the thing in action was the title to real estate; in four (*b, d, e, g*) the subject of the action was the right or liability arising under a contract. Of these four, however, but two (*d* and *e*) can properly be said to have been cases, in which the assignor of the right was dead, while in the other two (*b* and *g*) the deceased assignor was one whose *liability*, not whose property, was the subject of the action. We can then reach this conclusion, that the thing in action may be a right connected with property, either real or personal, which latter includes as well choses in action as those in possession, while the contract in action may be viewed either with respect to the right derived under it, or the liability imposed by it; and the assignor of either a right or a liability is one whose death excludes the operation of the act within the meaning of the proviso. In the case of torts, if the action is one which survives the death of the parties at all, the executor or administrator of the plaintiff or defendant must be substituted before the action can proceed, so that it will at once be brought within the clause relating to actions by or against executors or administrators.

Second, *as to the method of assignment.*—In the six cases in which the title to real estate formed the subject of the action, the right derived from the assignor was obtained in five different ways: (*a.*) Purchase at sheriff's sale; (*c* and *i.*) Descent; (*f.*) Deed from executor of decedent; (*h.*) Deed from decedent, with sundry mesne conveyances and sheriff's sale; and (*k*) Devise. In the remaining four cases (*b, d, e,* and *g*) the right or liability was cast upon the party to the action by mere operation of law, as the representative of the partnership; so that we find, that the term assignor cannot be used in any sense as relating to the mere voluntary transfer by assignment, technically so called, but that the assignment may be by any means whatever, whether by the act or agreement of the parties or by the mere operation of law, whereby one of the parties to the litigation represents, or claims to represent, the deceased person, either with respect to all or a part only of a right or liability, which is the immediate subject of the litigation. This is in keeping with the true spirit and intent of the act; and, bearing in mind that the liability under a contract may be quite as much the subject of assignment as the right, we are relieved of the difficulty which attended the discussion of the cases of deceased partners, where some confusion was occasioned by the introduction of questions as to the effect of the judgment upon the estate of the decedent, while in point of fact the real question was the effect of the judgment upon the surviving partner, who succeeded to the liability of the decedent, if any existed, and was bound to make it good out of the partnership assets if possible, thereby decreasing his own share, and out of his own property certainly, if the partnership assets were unequal to it. The test of this is the fact, that the proviso is for the protection of the party to the action, who may be a party either in his own right or the right of another. If suing or being sued in his own right, he is himself the object of protection; if in a representative capacity, then the estate or right which he represents in that suit is the object of protection; in either case the effect of the death of the person under whose right he attacks or defends is the thing to be guarded against; and so in the case of title to real estate it was unnecessary to inquire whether the deceased assignors had warranted, or whether the judgment could be used against their estates, *non constat*, that their estates would be affected at all; so in the case of bonds or personal property claimed through a decedent, the question is not whether the judgment can be used in a subsequent action on the decedent's warranty: the real point, and the only fact necessary to know, is that one who has stood in the line of title, under which one of the parties to the suit prosecutes or defends, is dead, and that the knowledge which he had, has died with him. But there must always, in the case of title to property, either real or personal, be a certain number of assignors, who have died; how are we to tell who is *the* assignor within the meaning of the proviso? The answer to this question will be found below in the answer to the second important question which it was said had arisen under the cases,—viz., as to what facts is the witness excluded from testifying? —and this bears as much upon the cases of executors and administrators as upon those in which the assignor is dead.

Third, *the extent to which the exclusion operates.*—It had been said, in *Karns* v. *Tanner*, (a)[1] "The true spirit of the proviso then

---

[1] P. 107.

seems to be that when a party to a thing or contract in action is dead, and his rights have passed, either by his own act or by that of the law, to another who represents his interest in the subject of controversy, the surviving party to that subject shall not testify to matters occurring in the lifetime of the adverse party, whose lips are now closed."

This language is plain enough; it does not say that the survivor shall not testify as to transactions with the decedent, but that he shall not testify as to "matters occurring in the lifetime of the adverse party." But, through an effort to make the actual working of the act entirely logical and reasonable, there arose, very early, a theory that the exclusion was only as to transactions with the decedent, while, at the same time, and, as it were, side by side with decisions upon this theory, there has always been a line of cases based upon the view indicated in that portion of the opinion quoted above.

In *Craig* v. *Brendel*, 19 Sm., 153 (October, 1871), which was an action of ejectment brought by Craig against Brendel for land purchased by Craig at sheriff's sale, under execution upon his own judgment against Brendel. The defence was, that the property belonged to Brendel's wife, under a previous conveyance. Before the trial the plaintiff had died, and his devisees were substituted on the record. In order to prove the purchase-money of the property to have been the wife's, the husband was called, and objected to because of the death of Craig. But it was held that he was properly admitted, because, *first*, he was "called to testify to no thing, contract, or transaction, to which he and the deceased, John Craig, were parties;" and, *second*, because his testimony was as "to matters to which he himself was no party in interest." Although the decision in *Watts* v. *Leidig*[1] was adverse to the admission of the witness, it will be remembered that it was placed upon the ground that the witness was substantially a party to the contract about which he offered to testify, and that as to that con-

---

[1] *Ante*, p. 104.

tract he was held incompetent, impliedly admitting that as to other matters he might be competent.

In *Pattison* v. *Armstrong*, 24 Sm., 476 (January, 1874), the plaintiff was held competent to testify, in ejectment, against the heirs of one Armstrong, the original defendant, as to the terms of a contract between him and one McGuier, the decedent's grantor, upon the ground that it was an offer "to prove a contract between parties both of whom are now living," and "the death of a subsequent and intervening purchaser, who was not a party to the contract," was insufficient to exclude.

In *McFerren* v. *Mont Alto Iron Co.*, 26 Sm., 180 (July 1874), there was an action of trespass *quare clausum fregit*; the subject of litigation was a right of way claimed by defendant and denied by the plaintiff. The grantor, under whom defendant claimed the right of way, was dead, but the plaintiff was held competent to testify as to transactions between himself and the grantor upon "matters having no connection with" his conveyance. WILLIAMS, J., said: "Surely the proviso was not intended to exclude parties from being witnesses, where the assignor of the thing or contract in action is dead, if they were not parties to the transaction, and are not called to testify to anything that took place between themselves and the deceased assignor."

Waltman v. *Herdic*, 9 N., 459 (June, 1879), was an action of ejectment for a small tract of land which was included in the warrant and survey under which the plaintiffs claimed, as well as that under which defendants claimed. B., whose estate still held the legal title to one-half of the land under the warrant under which plaintiffs claimed through him, was dead. T., one of the defendants, was offered as a witness to prove entry under the defendants' warrant, and subsequent possession, and title under the Statute of Limitations, but no transactions with B.; he was excluded. On writ of error by defendants, however, TRUNKEY, J., delivering the opinion of the court, said: "A grantor of the title on one side may be dead; if he had no transaction or communication of any kind with the adverse party, or one under whom he claimed, he is not an assignor in the meaning of the statute. Where there was no privity between the deceased assignor and the opposing party, as a general rule, the act applies. The converse is equally true. If nothing occurred, in the lifetime of the deceased, between him and the survivor, the case is unlike one where the subject is a contract. . . . The first thing that arrests attention is the absence of privity between Billman and Titus. There is no semblance of contract-relation. Nor are their respective titles links of the same chain. Before Billman had an interest in the Brady tract, while he lived, and since his death, Titus claimed the land in suit as part of the Hepburn warrant. The plaintiffs holding under Billman and others, demand nothing beyond the Brady survey. Aside from location of the original tract-line, Titus sets up title under the Statute of Limitations, the very nature of which excludes its derivation from Billman. There was no proposal to prove by Titus anything that Billman ever said or did, and plaintiffs point to nothing tending to show that there ever was any communication between them respecting the land. If the survivor is incompetent, where will competency begin when some grantor in the chain of title of the opposing party is dead? Can it be that if one party derives title through or under a deceased grantor, however remote, neither can be a witness? Proximity or remoteness of the deceased grantor is of no consequence, for the true inquiry is, has death sealed the lips of one party to a transaction of which both had knowledge?"

But compare with these decisions, and the arguments employed to sustain them, the decision in *Brady* v. *Reed*,[1] 6 N., 111 (May, 1878), where the plaintiff in an action against a firm, one of whom was dead, was held incompetent to testify as to anything which occurred in the lifetime of the decedent, although he had taken no part in the contract on which suit was brought. In *Hess* v. *Gour-*

[1] *Ante*, p. 112.

ley,[1] TRUNKEY, J., intimates that *Craig* v. *Brendel* is at variance with their decision; and *Ewing* v. *Ewing*[2] is a decision in which it was held to be error to have admitted as a witness one who claimed his title under adverse possession against the deceased assignor, although he carefully refrained from testifying as to any transaction or communication with the decedent, and "the very nature" of his title excluded the idea of its being derived from him. In *Brady* v. *Reed*, MERCUR, J., said: "It matters not that the offer be to prove a contract with the partner who is still living, when the effect is to charge the estate of the one who is dead. Although he may not personally have participated in the making of the contract, yet it does not follow, that if living he could not have testified to the fulfilment of it, or a subsequent release or discharge therefrom."

In *Ewing* v. *Ewing* the witness had "refrained from testifying in chief to any understanding or transaction between himself and his father in relation to the property;" and STERRETT, J., said: "His testimony as to the inception of his claim, and the character of his possession for a period of nearly thirty years, was clear and positive, and under the charge of the learned Judge must have satisfied the jury that his title under the statute, by adverse possession, was complete. If, under a proper construction of the Act, he was incompetent to prove what occurred in the lifetime of his father, it may be his misfortune; but the real or supposed hardship of any particular case cannot be considered in construing the statute."

A comparison of these two series of cases therefore forces us to the conclusion that the first proceeded upon a wrong theory in confining the exclusion to testimony as to particular facts; that they overlooked the fundamental principle of the proviso, which is intended to apply to *cases*, not to particular testimony, and which, without the aid of the act of 1870, would have absolutely

---

[1] *Ante*, p. 112.   [2] *Ante*, p. 113.

excluded a party from testifying as to anything whatever, and until a very recent act of May 11th, 1881, precluded persons in interest from opening their lips upon any subject.

But it is asked, who then is "the assignor of the thing or contract in action?" If *Pattison* v. *Armstrong*, and *Waltman* v. *Herdic* (*Craig* v. *Brendel* is omitted because the decision in that case may be sustained upon its second ground), are bad law and not reconcilable with the line of cases of which *Ewing* v. *Ewing* is the last, which literally and certainly in spirit follow the act, where are we to stop in the line of title? As was said in *Waltman* v. *Herdic,* "where will competency begin when some grantor in the chain of title of the opposing party is dead? Can it be that if one party derives title through or under a deceased grantor, however remote, neither can be a witness?" To this last question the answer must be, "Yes, if the deceased grantor claimed a title adverse to that set up by his grantee's or assignee's adversary." In other words, the assignor whose death absolutely closes the mouth of parties and interested persons, save as to facts subsequent to his death, is any person through whom one party to the action traces his title or his right, and who, if living, assuming the assignee's claim to be true, would stand in an adverse position to the other party. Thus if ejectment is brought by M. against N. upon a title derived through sundry mesne conveyances from B., and N. defends upon a title founded upon adverse possession against B. and his grantees; the death of A., B.'s grantor, affects the competency of neither of the parties, because neither of them claims under a title adverse to that of A., and no fact occurring in A.'s lifetime therefore could affect A.'s title, which is undisputed, but the death of C. or D., the intervening vendees under whom M. claims, excludes all testimony of facts prior to their respective deaths, although no communication with either of them was held by N. or any one under whom he claims to have acquired his title by adverse possession. Although not parties to a transaction about which the witness is offered to testify, it does not follow that they, since it was to their interest to protect the title, might not have ascertained or brought about other facts, by the evidence of which they would render the testimony of the proffered witness useless. If this theory is kept in view no real difficulty in determining the application of the proviso to the act can arise, although it is true that the reason for its application may in some cases seem slight; but the remedy for this lies with the legislature and not with the court.

Before we can have finally disposed of the question, however, we must observe certain other rules to be gathered from other cases, showing what an assignor is not rather than what he is.

(2.) *The assignor whose death excludes must be one who was himself beneficially interested prior to the assignment; if neither party claims title through him then his death renders neither of them incompetent.*

American Life Ins. & Trust Co. v. *Shultz*, 1 N. 46 (2 W. N. C., 665, May, 1876), was an action of assumpsit brought by Shultz to recover the value of a paid-up policy; under exception the plaintiff testified that by express contract with the agent of the company, who had since died, he could at the end of three years exchange his annual policy for one paid up. The verdict being for the plaintiff, the defendants took a writ of error, assigning as error the admission of the plaintiff to testify. The court held him competent, PAXSON, J., saying: "There is nothing in the Act of 15th April, 1869, which in terms excludes the plaintiff below as a witness. But it is contended that he comes within the spirit of the act, which was intended to produce equality and not to open the lips of one party while those of the other were closed. The answer to this is that the deceased person, Mr. Geiger, was not a party to the contract nor to this proceeding. He was merely the agent of the insurance company, and a competent witness prior to the act of 1869. Said act makes no one incompetent who was competent before. It was manifestly intended to enlarge, not to restrain, the admission of evidence." The practical effect of this decision, of course, is to render it impossible for a corporation ever to exclude the survivor of a contract, or one claiming under an adverse title by reason of the death of any of its officers or agents, with whom, indeed, the whole transaction may have taken place, but who, of course, would have acted only as agents.

Mann v. *Wieand*, 4 W. N. C., 6 (January, 1877), was an action of trespass on the case by the widow of Wieand to recover damages for the death of her husband, caused by the alleged negligence of the defendent in keeping vicious dogs, brought under the act of April 15th, 1851.[1] The defendant was offered as a witness, but rejected, and the verdict being for plaintiff, a writ of error was taken by the defendant. It was *held*, that the exclusion of the defendant was error, because the case was neither that of a deceased assignor, nor one by or against executors, administrators, or guardians.

Hostetter v. *Schalk*, 4 N., 220 (November, 1877), was an action of trover and conversion by Schalk against Hostetter to recover the value of 3000 barrels of oil. The plaintiffs brought in evidence that the oil had been purchased for them by one Hertz, since dead, as their agent, and that he transferred it in payment of his own indebtedness to the defendant. Hostetter was then called on his own behalf, but objected to by the plaintiffs on the ground of the death of Hertz, and excluded. The Supreme Court, however, held him entirely competent, PAXSON, J., saying, after quoting from the opinion in *Karns* v. *Tanner :* "This language manifestly refers to a contention between the survivor and the legal representatives of the deceased party to the contract, or those claiming through or under them. It is difficult to see how a stranger to the contract can object to the competency of the survivor as a witness. It does not produce the inequality referred to in Karns *v.* Tanner." These cases clearly support the proposition that no one who has not himself and in his own right been beneficially interested in the thing

---

[1] Purdon's Digest, 1093, pl. 2.

or contract in action can be considered as the assignor. This would seem to answer in the negative the question suggested before,[1] whether an executor or administrator can be regarded as an assignor. The beneficiaries derive their title not through *him*, but through his testator or intestate, by devise or devolution of law, and he and the new executor or administrator are but legal agents for them. And the next rule follows as a corollary to this.

(3.) *The mere fact of the witness having been a party to a transaction with a deceased assignor of one of the parties, or a decedent whose estate through a legal representative is a party to the record, is no ground for his exclusion, unless he is himself interested.*

The theory of the inequality of the parties has been so prominently brought forward in all of the decisions that the inequality has sometimes been urged as a ground of exclusion, even where a witness was not otherwise incompetent; but since the act was essentially an enabling act, the courts have rightly declined to recognize any such principle. In *Sheetz* v. *Hanbest's Exrs.*, 31 Sm., 100 (2 W. N. C., 637,[2] March, 1876), there was a feigned issue between Sheetz *et al.*, creditors of Lentz, as plaintiffs, and Hanbest as defendant, to try the validity of Hanbest's judgment against Lentz, and the question of fraud by Hanbest against Lentz in obtaining it. Hanbest died before trial, and his executors were substituted. The plaintiffs offered Lentz as a witness, but he was held incompetent, SHARSWOOD, J., saying that under *Ferree* v. *Thompson*, 2 Sm., 353,[3] he was disinterested, and therefore competent without recourse to the act, which was "intended as an enlarging statute. No person competent, before the passage of the act, was rendered thereafter incompetent, either by the words or the spirit of the law." To the same effect was the decision in *Vidal's Appeal*, 7 W. N. C., 159[4] (February, 1879), where, in the adjudication of the account of Wears *et al.*, executors of Whipper, the administrator of Annie M. Vidal presented several claims, aggregating $1875, and the

---

[1] *Ante*, p. 103.
[2] S. C., 9 Ph., 188.
[3] P. 157.
[4] S. C., 4 W. N. C., 527.

accountants offered Wears as a witness to prove that Mrs. Vidal had admitted to him that the decedent owed but $304. It was held on appeal from the Orphans' Court, that under the act of March 8th, 1865, the witness was rendered competent without regard to the act of 1869, and that it could not take away his competency.

(4.) *If the action is one by or against executors, administrators, or guardians, or the assignor of the thing or contract in action is dead, all parties and interested persons on both sides are incompetent to testify as to any facts prior to the death of the person whose estate is represented, or the assignor of one of the parties.*

Crouse v. *Staley*, 3 W. N. C., 83 (June, 1876), was a *sci. fa.* sur mortgage against Staley and wife; the property was the wife's; she died before trial, and her administrator was substituted as defendant. On the trial the plaintiff was offered as a witness and excluded, but the defendant, the husband, was admitted when offered for the defence. This was held to be error in the Supreme Court, where the exclusion was based upon the inequality of the parties; for while the plaintiff was excluded, it would have produced great inequality to permit the defendant, an interested party, to testify.[1] *Taylor* v. *Kelly*, 30 Sm., 95, decided that the act was nugatory in the case of husband and wife, when the facts brought it within the proviso, and MERCUR, J., said, "We must not overlook the fact that all competency imparted to any witness, by the enacting clause of the 1st sect., is entirely taken away by the proviso, in case an executor is a party to the action." The principle of the exclusion of the husband and wife was said by TRUNKEY, J., in *Hess* v. *Gourley*, 7 W. N. C., 157,[2] to be a doctrine "which rests upon the very letter and spirit of the proviso, which took out all actions therein described, instead of particular persons, from the operation of the Act of 1869." There is no

---

[1] This decision was also based upon the fact that as *husband* he could not testify, because the case was within the proviso to the act. See *postea*, p. 129.

[2] *Postea*, p. 129.

question, therefore, that when the proviso to the act applies at all, it excludes all parties and all interested persons. It is true that in *Gavit* v. *Supplee*, 2 W. N. C., 561 (March, 1876), where suit was brought by a surviving partner upon a contract made by his deceased partner, he was permitted to testify, but it was without objection, and the question of his competency was not raised in the Supreme Court. And in *Hostetter* v. *Schalk*,[1] where it was held that the deceased agent of the plaintiff, by whose assignment in his own right however the defendant claimed, was not an assignor whose death could close the mouth of the defendant, PAXSON, J., said, " Hertz is not an adverse party whose death closes the mouth of *either* party to the suit." But in that case there was at the time that the plaintiff testified, no evidence that the decedent bore any other relation than that of agent to any of the parties, and no objection to the plaintiff's competency was made; had it been made, based upon the fact that the deceased agent was assignor of the defendant, and that he claimed title through him in his own right, it is probable that the court would have sustained the objection. No other cases present any *dicta* at variance with this principle, and it is so obviously the proper and literal construction of the act, the enabling clause of which is not to apply at all in the excepted cases, that it would seem to need no further argument. One contingency presents itself, however. If the deceased person is the assignor of the plaintiff, it may happen, as it did in *Gavit* v. *Supplee*, that the defendant has made no objection to his testimony; will that render the defendant competent in his turn? Upon the authority of that case it will not. Therefore if there be any doubt as to the defendant's competency, but he is unwilling to raise it, he must run the risk of being excluded himself after the plaintiff's own testimony has been given, if, from fear of raising an objection which may exclude himself, he permits his adversary to testify.

On the other hand, if it is the death of the defendant's assignor

---

[1] *Ante*, p. 122.

or testator which excludes, he may waive the privilege of excluding his adversary, and render himself competent by permitting the plaintiff to testify, although without such waiver he would have been incompetent, because being himself the party for whose benefit the proviso exists, if he has seen fit to waive it, it cannot be taken advantage of by his adversary. There is no case which directly rules this point, but the facts are such as occurred in *Hostetter* v. *Schalk, supra* (4 N., 220).[1]

The Case of Husband and Wife under the Proviso.—*Whenever the action is one by or against executors, administrators, or guardians, or the assignor of the thing or contract in action is dead, neither husband nor wife is competent to testify in favor of the other, except as to facts subsequent to the death of the person whose death excludes.*

The decision in *Karns* v. *Tanner* was delivered in 1871, and it so strongly rested the importance of this clause of the proviso upon the ground of inequality, and the two distinct thoughts contained in the proviso, that subsequently it was forgotten that it applied to every part of the act alike, and its operation began to be limited only to cases in which parties to transactions with deceased persons were called, and thus inequality was produced, forgetting that the very language of the proviso placed all incompetency in the same category, and when it had any application it applied to all alike. We will trace the decisions in the case of husband and wife in their order, because the recent cases recognize the fact that the decisions on this point have been at variance. In 1870 an opinion was delivered in *Diehl* v. *Emig*, 15 Sm., 320 (1870), in which ejectment was brought by Diehl and wife, *in her right*, against Moul and the executors of John Emig; the trial took place prior to the act of April 9th, 1870, and the husband having been called as a witness was rejected. THOMPSON, C. J., said: "As the law stood the husband was not

---

[1] It may have been for this reason that the rule was refused in Kisterbock *v.* Harbeson, 1 W. N. C., 91 (D. C., November, 1874).

a competent witness, although he will be, we think, under the act above referred to, to prove anything occurring *since the decease of the decedent*, and that was what was proposed to be proved by him." This opinion clearly intimated that he would be incompetent to testify as to anything occurring *before* that time, but in 1872 was decided *Dellinger's Appeal*, 21 Sm., 425 (1872), an appeal from the Orphans' Court upon the audit of an executor's account. A claim had been presented against the estate by two claimants, who were themselves of course within the proviso, and incompetent, but under exception the wife of one and the husband of the other were permitted to testify. It was held, AGNEW, J., delivering the opinion, that they were competent, the court saying: " But the *witnesses*, as wife and husband, had no personal interest in this controversy, and were not parties to it. They were not to be excluded unless they fall within the first clause of the proviso prohibiting a husband or wife from testifying against each other. The witnesses being neither parties nor interested, their exclusion could rest only on the ground of policy. But this policy is removed by the enactment which declares that no policy of law shall exclude a person from being a witness in any civil proceeding, while the exception to the enactment does not embrace a husband and wife called to testify for each other." This view had previously been taken in *Craig* v. *Brendel*, 19 Sm., 153 (October, 1871)[1], where AGNEW, J., had said of the witness : " The only relation he bears to the case is that of husband of the contestant, the owner of the alleged title. But that relation is not within the proviso of the Act of 1869, for he is not called to testify *against* his wife."

Dellinger's Appeal seems to have been disregarded, however, in the Common Pleas of Philadelphia County, in May, 1875, where THAYER, P. J., held in *City, to use of Morris,* v. *Alsop*, 1 W. N. C., 473 (May, 1875), that the wife of the defendant, who was offered by the defence to prove certain matters occurring in the

---

[1] *Ante*, p. 116.

lifetime of the equitable plaintiff's testator, was incompetent. In the following November, *Taylor* v. *Kelly*, 30 Sm., 95 (3 W. N. C., 206, November, 1875), was argued. The action was *assumpsit* by William Kelly against Samuel Taylor, executor of Henry Barnes, deceased. The defendant, Taylor, was husband of the testator's daughter, who was one of the residuary legatees; he was offered as a witness and rejected, as was also the wife of Henry Barnes, another of the residuary legatees. The verdict was for the plaintiff, and the defendant took a writ of error, assigning for error the rejection of these proffered witnesses. The opinion of the court was delivered by MERCUR, J., who, after quoting the language of the proviso in full, proceeds: " Thus it appears the same imperative 'shall not apply' extends to a case in which an executor is a party, as to the prohibition of husband and wife from testifying against each other, and counsel to the privileged communication of his client. The language is neither doubtful nor obscure. Its clear and mandatory edict takes all these cases out of the statute. . . . . We must not overlook the fact that all competency imparted to any witness, by the enacting clause of the 1st sect., is entirely taken away by the proviso, in case an executor is a party to the action. It would be no more clearly in the face of the statute to hold that husband and wife may testify against each other, than that they may testify in their own favor, when an executor is a party to the action, to events which transpired during the life of the testator. Each is prohibited by the same expressive language. The same clause in the enactment made both husband and wife equally competent. The same prohibition in the proviso made them both incompetent to testify in behalf of each other when an executor is a party. . . . The conclusion to which we have arrived is sustained by Diehl *v.* Emig, 15 P. F. Smith, 320. That was an action by a daughter against the executor of her father's will. It was held her husband was not a competent witness to testify to matters occurring in her father's lifetime. It is also in accord with the spirit and reasoning of Karns v. Tanner, 16 P. F. Smith 297, and of Pattison v. Armstrong et al., 24 Id. 476. It is true the conclusion to which we have arrived is in conflict with Dellinger's Appeal, 21 P. F. Smith, 425; but a more careful examination of the act convinces us that due consideration was not then given to its provisos." AGNEW, C. J., and SHARSWOOD, J., dissented from this opinion,[1] and WILLIAMS, J., was absent, but this left a majority of four to two, and the decision has since been affirmed. At the same time that this case was under consideration, there was a similar case before the court, *Stoll* v. *Weidman*, 3 W. N. C., 205, in which the same point arose, the wife of a plaintiff having been admitted, and a reargument upon it was ordered; but the decision in *Taylor* v. *Kelly* having been delivered on November 22d, on November 24th "the order for the reargument was countermanded, and a *venire facias de novo* awarded." In *Crouse* v. *Staley*, 3 W. N. C., 83 (June, 1876), which was a *sci. fa.* sur mortgage against Staley and wife,—the property was the wife's,—she died before trial, and her administrator was substituted; it was held that by the death of the wife the plaintiff was necessarily excluded as to facts previous thereto, and that for the sake of equality the husband of the defendant was likewise incompetent.[2]

In *Hess* v. *Gourley*, 7 W. N. C., 157 (March, 1879),[3] TRUNKEY, J., said: "Inasmuch as *Craig* v. *Brendel* (19 P. F. Smith, 153) was not alluded to, it is suggested that, upon its authority, Peter Hess was a competent witness for his wife, and it seems to support the position, but, if such be its bearing, it is at variance with the doctrine in Taylor v. Young. That doctrine rests upon the very letter and spirit of the proviso, which took out all actions therein described, instead of particular persons, from the operation of the Act of 1869. . . . . The power which in 1878 made surviving

---

[1] For the dissenting opinion see 3 W. N. C., 206.

[2] See also following, *Taylor* v. *Kelly*, Bierly's Appeal, 3 W. N. C., 210 (May, 1876), and Watson's Est., 3 W. N. C., 244 (O. C., Oct., 1877).

[3] *Ante*, p. 112.

partners competent in certain cases, can make husband and wife competent to any extent deemed expedient, as to matters which took place before the death of the assignor of the thing or contract in suit."

The foregoing decisions leave no manner of doubt now that the proviso applies as well to the case of husband and wife as it does to any other.

Indeed, since the act of April 9th, 1870, was held to apply only to parties,[1] it follows as a curious result that a wife would not be competent even as to facts subsequent to the death of the person whose death excluded, but the husband would, because he would be a necessary party to any suit in which she was a party, while she would not be a party to his suits. This, however, is no longer an open question, since the act of May 11th, 1881, places all interested persons in the same category as parties with respect to the privileges secured by the act of 1870.[2]

The Case of Infamous Persons Under the Proviso.—As the removal of the incompetency of infamous persons by the act seems never to have been adverted to, the question of the effect of the existence of the conditions of the proviso upon such cases has likewise never been decided. There is logically, however, no reason for distinguishing such a case from that of husband and wife, and it may be presumed that if the opinion heretofore expressed[3] is correct, that the enabling clause removed the incompetency arising from infamy, its effect is excluded in cases coming within the terms of the proviso. The effect of the enabling legislation upon the general policy of the law, as growing out of the policy of exclusion from interest, is discussed hereafter.[4]

---

[1] Whitney v. Shippen, 2 W. N. C., 470 (March, 1876), *postea*, p. 131.
[2] *Postea*, p. 155.   [3] *Ante*, p. 90.   [4] *Postea*, p. 159.

CHAPTER VI.

THE ACT OF APRIL 9TH, 1870, AND THE EXCEPTION TO THE PROVISO OF THE ACT OF 1869.

The Act of April 9th, 1870, § 1.[1]—The text of this act was given at the same time with that of the act of 1869, because it so soon followed it as really to be regarded as a part of the first act in interpreting it. It was said in one of the lower courts, apparently before this act was passed, that an administratrix, the wife of the intestate, was competent to testify as to facts subsequent to the death of her husband;[2] but this could not be sustained under the Act of 1869 alone.[3] It is immaterial, however, since the act of 1870 renders all *parties* competent to testify as to facts or transactions occurring since the death of the person whose estate is the subject of litigation.[4] This is confined to parties, however, and one incompetent from interest, but not a party, was not rendered competent by the act.[5] The benefit of this act has, however, recently been extended to interested persons as well as to parties.[6]

Testimony of any facts existing subsequent to the death of the person whose estate through a legal representative is a party to the record is competent, notwithstanding it may tend to show the existence of the same, or of other facts prior to his death.

In *Long* v. *Spencer*, 28 Sm., 303 (1 W. N. C., 435, May, 1875), assumpsit was brought on a promissory note by Long, administrator

---

[1] Purdon's Digest, 625, pl. 20; *ante*, p. 85.

[2] Cawley *v.* Wilson, 7 Ph. 676 (C. P. Northampton Co.).

[3] Crouse *v.* Staley, *ante*, p. 129.

[4] Diehl *v.* Emig, 15 Sm., 320. Rutherford's Est., 2 W. N. C., 493 (O. C., March, 1876).

[5] Whitney *v.* Shippen, 2 W. N. C., 470 (March, 1876); Whitney *v.* Shippen, 8 N. 22 (February, 1879).

[6] Act May 11th, 1881, P. L.; *postea*, p. 155.

d. b. n. of Cottrell, against Spencer & Co. The letters of the former administrator had been revoked. The note had not been stamped, as required by the United States internal revenue laws, until, within a few days before the trial it was done at the request of the plaintiff by the Collector of Internal Revenue in accordance with the act. Under exception Spencer and Newton, two of the defendants, were permitted to testify that the former administrator had admitted that the note was unstamped when it came into his possession; but on writ of error, GORDON, J., delivering the opinion of the court, said: "This testimony *went to prove that the note was unstamped, or the stamp uncancelled, when passed to Cottrell;* as, however, this evidence was of matter occurring before his death, and which, if alive, he might have rebutted by his own testimony, it comes within the proviso of the Act of 1869, and should have been excluded." This decision is doubtless correct, because of the irrelevancy of the evidence, but, as might have been supposed, the reason assigned for it, which may now be regarded as a *dictum*, was repudiated, although the case was not referred to in the argument nor the opinion in the subsequent case of *Rothrock* v. *Gallaher*, 10 N., 108 (October, 1879), which was an action of trover and conversion by Rothrock, executor of Gallaher, deceased, to use, etc., against Jane Gallaher for some bonds. The defendant was permitted to testify that the package in which the bonds were supposed to be was in the same condition when opened by one of the witnesses as it was in "from and immediately after the death of" the intestate. The verdict and judgment were for the defendant. On writ of error, taken by the plaintiff, the court said, MERCUR, J., delivering the opinion: "The act of 9th April, 1870, makes the defendant competent to testify 'to matters occurring since the death of the person whose estate, through a legal representative, is a party to the record.' It fixes no period of time after his death, when the matters shall have occurred, whether they be immediately thereafter or whether months or years have intervened; the defendant is thereby made competent to testify in regard to them.

She is not made incompetent to testify to any fact occurring or existing after the death of the decedent, *by reason that her testimony may inferentially tend to prove the same facts existed prior to his death.*"[1]

This case is within both the letter and the spirit of the act, and clearly supports the proposition.

The exception to the *proviso :*

"**Excepting in issues and . inquiries** *devisavit vel non* **and others, respecting the right of such deceased owner, between parties claiming such right by devolution on the death of such owner.**"

The cases upon this exception are not very numerous, but they are interesting in so far as the practical effect of the literal interpretation of the language is to do away, in certain cases, with the principle supposed to have governed in framing the proviso. The reason for the broad exception is seen at a glance, for in every issue *devisavit vel non* the assignor of the thing or right in action about the title to which the claim exists must be dead, yet neither party to the issue stands in an adverse position to the right of such assignor, as in the case where there is a common assignor whose rights have fallen upon one or both of the parties to the action prior to his death ; on the contrary were he alive no claim to those rights would exist at all. It therefore seems proper that an exception should be made in a case where all of the parties are on an equal footing, and the interest of the deceased assignor, were it possible to obtain his evidence, would be *in equilibrio*. The same reason applies to other inquiries respecting the right of such deceased owner, between parties claiming such right by devolution on the death of such owner, for by devolution must be meant the act of law as distinguished from the act of the parties, and as between two volunteers, contestants for the same right belonging to the decedent, his evidence, if obtainable, would be no more likely to con-

---

[1] *Cf.* Emig *v.* Diehl, 26 Sm., 362.

tradict one than the other. The first case under this exception was *Bowen* v. *Goranflo*, 23 Sm., 357 (May, 1873), in which in an issue *devisavit vel non* the executor, who was also a devisee, was held competent to testify in support of the will, MERCUR, J., saying: "This is an issue *devisavit vel non*. It is between parties claiming a right by devolution on the death of the former owner. The subject-matter is respecting the right so acquired. Thus the form of the suit, the parties thereto, and the subject-matter bring it within the exception. We see nothing in it to exclude a party who is either devisee or executor only."

In 1876 *Camp* v. *Stark*, 2 W. N. C., 577, held the act to be inoperative to enable a devisee to prove the will of a married woman who died before its passage, although the will was not offered for probate until afterwards. The reason given is that the act requires the will of a married woman to be executed in the presence of two "competent witnesses," *i. e.*, competent at the time of its execution. This rule, therefore, would apply to the case of any married woman's will made prior to the date of the act, whether she died before or after its passage. But in the case of any other testator it would not, because the witnesses need only be competent at the time of probate. The decision of this case, of course, had no bearing upon the construction of the exception itself, but in the same year it was again brought directly before the court, and *Bowen* v. *Goranflo* was affirmed by an equally divided court. The case was *Frew* v. *Clark*, 3 W. N. C., 497 (Jan., 1876). There were three questions involved: 1st. Whether the paper offered for probate was a testamentary paper. 2d. Whether the legatee was a competent witness to prove it. 3d. Whether this very devisee had not used undue influence in procuring the paper. The devisee had been permitted to testify, and the verdict and judgment were in his favor. The judgment on the question of the admission of the devisee was affirmed on the authority of *Bowen* v. *Goranflo*, SHARSWOOD and PAXSON, JJ., dissenting, and AGNEW, C. J., doubting the correctness of the earlier authority. A reargument was ordered upon the single question of the admission of Clark, the legatee, as a witness. It was urged that the clause was to be read as a whole; that in order to bring a case within the exception there must be (1) an issue or inquiry, either *devisavit vel non* or otherwise, respecting the right of the deceased owner, (2) between parties claiming that right, and (3) both of the contending parties must claim by devolution on the death of such owner. But an issue or inquiry *devisavit vel non* is a well-known form of action to test the simple question of the existence of a legally operative testamentary paper, under which one of the contestants claims title; such an inquiry therefore can never be between parties all of whom claim by devolution, if by devolution is meant the act of law as distinguished from the voluntary act of an assignor or testator. The natural interpretation, and the one put upon it by the court at the first argument, is clearly the right one. The proviso had excluded from the operation of the act actions by or against executors, administrators, or guardians, and those in which the assignor was dead, because it was thought to be unfair that one party should be permitted to testify in his own favor, while the other was cut off from obtaining the testimony of a person who had preceded him in the line of title, and who if alive would be standing in his shoes and with an interest in his favor; but when all hands were simply fighting over the dead man's purse, no one of them could lay claim to the benefit of his testimony, because if he were alive the fight couldn't go on at all; nobody, therefore, would be injured by his absence, and consequently the testimony of none of the parties could put the others to the disadvantage which was contemplated by the act. It is possible that an actual inequality may be produced by this construction, but the court has no more right to remedy this by a decision not warranted by the act, than it had to interpret the first part of the proviso in accordance with its views as to what the law ought to be rather than the language which said what the law was. This is an enabling act, and an exception to it must be construed strictly. On the second argument, owing to the absence of WILLIAMS, J., the court was equally divided, and the former judgment was therefore reaffirmed.

Under these circumstances it would seem that on the authorities the question is almost an open one still, for should it arise soon again, as it inevitably will, the court might without impropriety reconsider its last decision. At the same time, strong as are the reasons urged by the dissenting opinion in this case, the judgment certainly followed the act. MERCUR, J., said, after referring to the former decision: "A careful review of the act confirms us in the correctness of the conclusion at which we then arrived. We do not see how effect can otherwise be given to the clause in question. It is claimed, however, that this construction of the statute will open the door to fraud and perjury. It may be so. It is possible that permitting parties to testify in any case has caused much perjury. . . . If the evil preponderates in obeying its mandates, the corrective power is lodged in the Legislature to modify or repeal what they have enacted."[1]

An instance of the second class of cases is found in *Greenawalt* v. *McEnelley*, 4 N., 352 (Nov., 1877), which was an action of ejectment; the plaintiffs claimed as collateral heirs of one Guffey deceased, and the defendant as his daughter. On the trial defendant's mother, in order to prove the defendant's legitimacy, was permitted under objection to testify to the fact of her marriage with the decedent. On writ of error to the verdict and judgment for defendant taken by the plaintiffs, PAXSON, J., delivering the opinion of the court, said: "We need not discuss the question whether Margaret Gilson would have been a competent witness prior to the act of April 15th, 1869, Pamph. L. 30. That act clearly made her competent, this being a contest between parties claiming the estate of Benjamin Guffey, her deceased husband, by devolution." It has been already noticed that this case also de-

---

[1] See also Hopple's Est., 3 W. N. C., 79 (O. C., Oct., 1876).

cided that in such issues and inquiries the testimony of the wife is not against the husband within the meaning of the act.[1]

Another point was urged in *Hopple's Est.*, 3 W. N. C., 79 (O. C., October, 1876), that this exception did not apply to proceedings before an examiner on appeal from the register, who refused an issue because, it was said, this was merely a preliminary examination, and not an issue at all. But it was an "inquiry," and more than that, it would be an anomaly for one to be competent at the final trial of a cause, and yet incompetent at a preliminary examination for the information of the court. The converse of this had always been the rule in ordinary cases with regard to parties and interested witnesses, who were usually competent then, although incompetent in a subsequent trial.[2]

A possible question may arise upon the meaning of the words " other issues and inquiries between parties claiming such right by devolution on the death of such deceased owner." By devolution in this connection may be meant only the act of law, or it may mean any method by which, *at the death* of the owner, his rights fall upon another, *e. g.*, in a devise to " children," a feigned issue may be awarded to test the legitimacy of one claiming to be included in the devise. It is possible that some argument might be made as to the literal meaning of the term devolution (the case is certainly not an issue *devisavit vel non*), but the spirit and reason of the exception are so absolutely at variance with such a narrow construction as to permit a breadth of interpretation in this, which is an enabling act, which certainly would cover such a case. There is in the relative position of the parties no difference between this and the case of *Greenawalt* v. *McEnelley*.

[1] *Ante*, p. 97.   [2] *Ante*, p. 41.

CHAPTER VII.

THE SECOND AND THIRD SECTIONS OF THE ACT OF APRIL 15TH, 1869.

THE second and third sections of the Act of April 15th, 1869, provide:

"Section 2. That a party to the record of any civil proceeding in law or equity, or a person for whose immediate benefit such proceeding is prosecuted or defended, may be examined as if under cross-examination, at the instance of the adverse party, or any of them, and for that purpose may be compelled, in the same manner, and subject to the same rules for examination, as any other witness, to testify; but the party calling for such examination shall not be concluded thereby, but may rebut it by counter-testimony.

"Section 3. That the testimony of witnesses authorized by this act may be had by deposition or commission issued, as the case may require, with such notice to the party to be examined, and to the adverse party, as is now or may hereafter be prescribed by the rules of the proper court, touching the taking of depositions and testimony on commission."[1]

The Second Section.—*A witness called under the second section of the act is to be considered in all respects as if originally offered and examined on his own behalf.*

It will be at once observed that in the second section the language used is not unlike that of the act of March 8th, 1865, except that a party when called under the act of 1869 "may be examined as if under cross-examination," and that the party calling the witness is not concluded by his testimony, but may contradict

---

[1] Purdon's Digest, 624, pl. 17, 18.

it. How much liberty is granted in conducting such an examination is explained in *Brubaker* v. *Taylor*, 26 Sm., 83 (May, 1874), in which the defendant called the plaintiff under this act. After additional testimony had been given by another witness, the plaintiff was recalled and asked whether she had not made, at a previous time, declarations inconsistent with her present story. To these questions the plaintiff's counsel objected, and the objection was sustained. The verdict and judgment being for plaintiff, the defendant took a writ of error, assigning for error, *inter alia*, the exclusion of these questions. In delivering the opinion of the court, which reversed the judgment, SHARSWOOD, J., said: "When the plaintiff below was called to the stand as a witness by the defendants they had a right to examine her as if under cross-examination—put to her leading questions—and draw from her any facts or admissions which would corroborate their own case or weaken hers. . . . It is evident that she was to be considered in all respects as if originally offered and examined as a witness in her own behalf."

(1.) *Who May be Called Under this Section.*—The decisions under the act of 1865 furnish us much light for interpreting this section, on other points their language is so similar,—" any party in any civil action or proceeding, whether at law or in equity, may compel any adverse party or any person for whose immediate and adverse benefit," etc., is that of the former. The purpose of the enactment in the act of 1869 is clear enough; it is that those persons who originally enjoyed the privilege of refusing to testify against themselves, and who, by the act of 1865, were made subject to an examination in chief by the adverse party, might now be called as if under cross-examination also; and those persons we saw in considering the former act are actually or substantially parties with an interest adverse to the party thus calling them.[1] The new element introduced by the more recent act is the possibility of getting under

---

[1] *Ante*, p. 79. Hogeboom's Exr. *v.* Gibbs et al., 7 N., 235; Guldin *v.* Guldin, 10 W. N. C., 395.

cross-examination a witness competent in his own behalf under the enabling clause of the act, who before would not have been privileged from being a witness at all if his adversary had chosen to call him, but whose testimony would have been binding. This could not have been the intention of the legislature, and it is therefore particularly important to observe that only those actually or substantially parties are within its meaning; and for the protection of others interested, not even those actually parties can be called under this act or that of 1865, if they are interested in favor of the party calling them.

By the same argument from analogy to the act of 1865 we may conclude that the decision in *O'Rourke* v. *McGrath*, 1 Brews., 302 (Jan., 1867),[1] is equally applicable here, and that under it the wife of a party is not liable to be called; but probably the husband would be, for he is always a party when she is, and he is, to the extent of the costs of the suit at least, a party with an interest adverse to her opponent.

(2.) *Application of this Section to Divorce Proceedings.*—Another interesting point arises here, whether, in divorce proceedings, the libellant or respondent can call the other under this section of the act of 1869. In *Bronson* v. *Bronson*, 8 Ph., 261 (C. P., 1871), the respondent added to the list of witnesses attached to her cross-interrogatories the name of the libellant, and the court, before whom the question arose, LUDLOW, J., delivering the opinion, ruled that this could not be done. The argument in the opinion is made to turn upon the act of March 4th, 1870, by which husband and wife are made competent to testify against each other in divorce suits,[2] and it is said that because this was an *enabling* act it could not be used to take away a privilege. But it was not necessary to refer to this act at all; the husband was not called to testify against his wife. The act of 1865 had authorized "any party in any civil action or proceeding, whether at law or in equity," within

[1] *Ante*, p. 80.   [2] *Postea*, p. 151.

which category surely proceedings for divorce must come, to call the adverse party, and the second section of the act of 1869 had said that "a party to the record of any civil proceeding in law or equity might be examined as if under cross-examination," so that there was no necessity for appealing to the act of 1870 at all. In this case no intention of calling the libellant under the act of 1869 appeared, so that if compelled to testify at all it would have been under the act of 1865; but the argument employed by the court fails to show satisfactorily that this could not have been done. If one of the parties to such proceedings can be compelled to testify under the first act, there is the more reason for holding such a case to be within the operation of the second. Prior to the act of 1869, of course, the act of 1865 would have been of no avail, because testimony obtained in this way would have been either for or against the husband or wife, but when this act removed the incompetency of both so far as to permit the testimony of either in favor of the other, the only argument which might have been made against this construction, prior to the act of March 4th, 1870, was that possibly in this way either husband or wife might be compelled to testify *against* the other on cross-examination, but this we have already seen could not operate to prevent the benefit of the act being obtained.[1] This case has been referred to at length because it is believed to have regulated the practice in divorce suits to some extent, and since it was not appealed from, and the decision has therefore not received the sanction of the Supreme Court, it seemed not without value to point out the possible error into which the court may have fallen. If this decision should prove to be erroneous, then either husband or wife can be called in divorce proceedings by the other side, but of course no confidential communications can be disclosed.[2]

(3.) *The Application of this Section to Cases not within the Enabling Clause.*—Whether this section of the act applies to those cases

---

[1] *Ante*, p. 93. [2] *Ante*, p. 97.

to which the first section of the act is inapplicable has never been authoritatively decided. It was said in *Hyneman's Est.*, 2 W. N. C., 571 (O. C., May, 1876),[1] that the second section of the act is inapplicable in all cases in which the first does not apply; but this view is opposed to the common practice of the lower courts, and places too wide a construction upon the words of the proviso, that "this *act* shall not apply," etc., which clearly refers to the enabling clause, which immediately precedes, and cannot fairly be presumed to apply to a subsequent section, the very nature of which is quite distinct from the class of cases excluded. The statement was unnecessary for the decision of the case in which it was made, which was rightly decided on other grounds, and if reviewed would probably now be modified. There seems to be no reason why this section is not intended to operate in all cases, whether the first section is applicable or not, for it commences as upon an entirely new subject, and applies to a party to the record of "any civil proceedings."

(4.) *The Degree of Credibility Conferred by Calling a Witness under the Second Section.*—We may next consider the effect of calling as a witness under this act one who would otherwise be incompetent. We saw that the effect of calling an adverse party under the act of 1865 was to give him credibility, which would enable him to testify on his own behalf so long as the party calling him remained alive,[2] and the inquiry naturally suggests itself whether such is the case when he is called under the act of 1869. Whether, for instance, as in the case of *Seip* v. *Storch*,[3] a party can call his adversary and ask him questions on certain points, omitting others which, in the opinion of the party calling, it might be unwise to touch upon; and the witness then be unable to testify on his own behalf upon all points which he may deem material. The rule adopted in *Seip* v. *Storch* was founded upon the theory that the fact of calling the adverse party as one's own witness of itself

---

[1] S. C., 11 Ph., 135.   [2] *Ante*, p. 75.   [3] 2 Sm., 210.

stamped him with credibility, and that his adversary should not be permitted to give him credibility as to some facts and deny it as to others. The presumption is entirely different, however, when a party or interested person is called under the act of 1869. The very fact of calling him as if under cross-examination precludes the idea of credibility, and the fact of cross-examination precludes the idea of making him the witness of the party by whom he is called. This view finds some support in *Bierly's Appeal*, 3 W. N. C., 210 (May, 1876), where a party called by his adversary to testify as to matters subsequent to the death of the assignor was held incompetent to testify for himself as to matters prior to that time.[1] The design of the law would seem to be simply the withdrawal of the privilege theretofore given of remaining silent in one's own case.

(5.) *The Credibility of Co-plaintiffs or Co-defendants of Parties called under the Second Section.*—Obviously the act of April 10th, 1867, rendering competent co-plaintiffs or co-defendants of parties called under the act of 1865, has no application to those who may be called under this section of the act of 1869, for the act of 1867 refers in terms to that of 1865, to which it is a supplement. No other legislation covers the case, and there seems to be no doubt that whatever effect may be given to the calling of one of the parties under this section, no credibility is thereby given to his co-plaintiffs or defendants.

The Third Section.—This has given rise to several interesting points, and in passing there should be noticed its use in connection with the second section. Under the rules of Court of Philadelphia County the deposition of any witness may be taken upon eight days' notice, so that in case of death or inability to attend the trial, the benefit of the witness's testimony may be obtained. In 1877, in *Yerkes* v. *Whitaker*, 4 W. N. C., 429, 571, the defendant was subpœnaed by the plaintiff under a rule to take his depo-

---

[1] Br's., Tr. & H., § 644.

sition, and upon his declining to answer, the facts were certified to the court (C. P. 3), by whom a rule for an attachment was made absolute, but subsequently rescinded, the court remarking that they would require an affidavit setting forth the reasons and the proposed line of examination. In the meantime the Common Pleas No. 2 had discharged a similar rule upon the ground that, while the case was within the letter of the act, the rule of court was not intended to compel a party to submit to a mere fishing examination;[1] but Common Pleas No. 1 had made the rule absolute.[2] The result of this diversity of opinion between courts of co-ordinate jurisdiction was the passage of the following amendment to the rules of court permitting the taking of depositions on eight days' notice:[3] "But no party shall be entitled to compel the deposition of the adverse party, in advance of the trial, except upon an order of the Court, upon notice and cause shown."[4] The courts thus virtually adopted the rule laid down for its own action by Common Pleas No. 3 in *Yerkes* v. *Whitaker.*

The other cases on the third section are in a regularly progressive series, each founded upon the previous decision and proceeding further in its results. The outcome of them is that—

(1.) *Properly verified notes of testimony, or the deposition of a witness rendered competent by legislation, taken at a time when he was competent, are competent evidence in a subsequent trial of the same cause, or in another cause between the same parties or their legal representatives, involving the same point in issue, if the witness is dead or has subsequently become incompetent, either from interest or any other cause.*

The first case is that of *Evans's Admx.* v. *Reed*, 2 W. N. C., 175 (November, 1875), which was an action of account render

---

[1] Asch v. Pass. R. W. Co., 4 W. N. C., 571 (C. P. 2, December, 1877).

[2] Wise v. Dispensary, 4 W. N. C., 570 (C. P. 1, 1877).

[3] Rule XV, § 48.

[4] 5 W. N. C., 14.

brought by Evans against Reed. The trial took place in 1872, at which time the testimony of both plaintiff and defendant was taken; there was a verdict for plaintiff, which was set aside. Before the second trial Evans had died, and his administratrix was substituted as party on the record, and the form of action changed to assumpsit. On the second trial the plaintiff offered in evidence the judge's notes of the testimony of Evans, taken on the former trial, to be verified by the oath of the judge; they were objected to and excluded. The verdict and judgment were for defendant, but on writ of error taken by plaintiff it was *held* that the testimony was admissible, MERCUR, J., saying: "The third section of the Act of 15th April, 1869, permitting parties to testify, expressly declares the testimony of witnesses authorized by the act may be had 'by deposition or commission issued.' The manifest intent then was to permit the deposition of a party to be taken for the perpetuation of his testimony against all contingencies that might arise—whether of absence or of death. The Act of 28th March, 1814 (Purd. Dig. 625, pl. 24), declares 'any deposition taken or to be taken in any cause, [which] by the rules of law, may be read in evidence on the trial of the cause in which it is or may be taken shall be allowed to be read in evidence in any subsequent cause wherein the same matter shall be in dispute between the said parties or persons, their heirs, executors, administrators or assign[ee]s.' If the deposition of a party be duly and regularly taken so as to be admissible in evidence in a pending case, it is very clear that it would be admissible in a subsequent suit between the administrators of the parties involving the same subject-matter. If admissible in a subsequent suit, it must certainly be in the case in which it was taken. . . . . When the plaintiff in this case testified, he was unquestionably competent. His testimony then became a part of the evidence in the case. If the second trial had taken place in his lifetime, he being at the time out of the jurisdiction of the Court, or unable by reason of sickness to be present, his testimony could have been read in evidence. So for a like reason it may be after his death. The evidence was not taken in an action in which, at the time, any executor, administrator, or guardian was a party."

Speyerer & Co. v. *Bennett's Exrs.*, 29 Sm., 445 (November, 1875), did not differ from *Evans* v. *Reed*, except that in it was offered a deposition regularly taken instead of the notes of testimony, and on the authority of the former case it was held to have been properly admitted. In this case, however, was suggested, though not decided, the competency of the living party to testify in rebuttal of the deposition; but this very point arose and was decided in *Pratt* v. *Patterson*, 31 Sm., 114 (3 W. N. C., 161, May, 1876). In this case another important point also was decided. The defendant had died. On the trial the plaintiff offered himself as a witness and was excluded. He then offered the notes of his testimony, given in the lifetime of the defendant, in a former action between the same parties, which had been discontinued: the defendant had been examined at the same time: this also was excluded. A nonsuit was entered, and on writ of error it was *held:* (1.) That on the authority of *Evans* v. *Reed*, the *notes* of testimony were admissible. (2.) The oral testimony of the plaintiff was rightly excluded. On the first point MERCUR, J., said: "This evidence was taken on due notice, with ample opportunity for cross-examination. It was not testimony that could have been fabricated after the death of the party whose interest might be injuriously affected thereby. When taken the parties stood on an equal footing. Each had the right to perpetuate his own testimony. Each availed himself of that right. All statutes which provide for the perpetuation of evidence are in furtherance of justice and a due administration of the law. They should receive a liberal construction. This is not the case of a deposition of a person taken when he was not interested, but becomes so before it was offered in evidence. Here he was no more interested when his testimony was offered than when it was first taken. His interest had remained unchanged."

In *Hays's Appeal*, 10 N., 265 (January, 1880), a bill in equity for a partnership account had been filed. Upon the hearing before the master the plaintiff was offered as a witness in his own behalf, and pending his examination in chief the defendant died. At the next meeting, after the appointment of the defendant's administrator, a motion was made on his behalf to strike out the testimony of the plaintiff, which was refused by the master, because "at the time it was given and reduced to writing it was legitimate testimony, and because the defence had sufficient time and opportunity to cross-examine the plaintiff, and have the testimony of the defendant taken." It seems from the opinion that the plaintiff offered himself for cross-examination after the appointment of the defendant's administrator. On appeal, it was said by the court as to this point, STERRETT, J., delivering the opinion: "When the plaintiff testified he was undoubtedly a competent witness, and nothing that occurred thereafter would have justified the court or master in excluding his testimony. . . . . It was not the fault of the plaintiff that defendant, by reason of sickness, was prevented from being present in person to cross-examine, or to testify in his own behalf. During the lifetime of the original parties, they were both competent witnesses, and either had a right to testify or have his testimony perpetuated, so that it might be used in the event of sickness or death."

It would seem that the admissibility of such testimony is not confined to the incompetency caused by death, either his own or that of his adversary; but if, as all of the preceding cases rule, such testimony is to be treated as that of any other witness, then incompetency arising from loss of memory, insanity, or absence from the jurisdiction is sufficient to admit it: *Rothrock* v. *Gallaher*, 10 N., 108 (October, 1879).[1]

(2.) *The admission of the deposition or notes of previous testimony of one of the parties does not render the adverse party competent.*

---

[1] *Cf.* Riegel v. Wilson, 10 Sm., 388 (February, 1869); Emig v. Diehl, 26 Sm., 359 (July, 1873).

In 1877 *Evans's Admx.* v. *Reed* (4 W. N. C., 301),[1] came before the court a second time. On the third trial the notes of testimony of Evans had been put in evidence, and the defendant was then permitted to testify on his own behalf upon the theory of equality, which was thought to be violated otherwise; but the Supreme Court, on the authority of *Pratt* v. *Patterson*,[2] held him incompetent, because "it by no means follows that because the testimony of the deceased party, duly taken in his lifetime, was given in evidence on the trial, therefore the surviving party is made competent to go on the stand to testify in his own behalf. When the testimony of the party, since deceased, was taken, he was a competent witness. He was subject to cross-examination by the opposite party. The lips of the survivor were not then closed. He could then have offered himself as a witness to explain or contradict the testimony of the opposite party. If he did so, he thereby perpetuated his own testimony, and it is now available. If he then failed to perpetuate it, there is no equality in now permitting him, after the death of his adversary, to go on the stand to testify to anything which transpired during the life of the opposite party. The lips now closed in death, cannot prompt any cross-examination, nor explain or contradict the testimony thus given." Of course no inference can be drawn from these decisions that the deposition of a person incompetent at the time that it is taken is any more competent than that person himself would be to testify orally.[3]

(3.) *Admissibility on his own Behalf of Notes of Testimony or Deposition of Witness called by the adverse party for Cross-examination.*— Other analogies to the act of 1865 suggest themselves here, and amongst them the admissibility on his own behalf of the testimony or deposition of a witness called under this section of the act for cross-examination, offered in a subsequent suit, when he

---

[1] *Ante,* p. 144.   [2] *Ante,* p. 146.
[3] Wheeler's Est., 8 W. N. C., 534 (O. C., July, 1880).

is absent from the trial or incompetent to testify for himself. Of course if in a subsequent suit both parties are alive and present at the trial, they are both competent for themselves, and either may be called by the other for cross-examination; but in case the one party has died, which will, of course, render the other incompetent, may the survivor put in evidence the notes of his own testimony taken as if under cross-examination, or does the rule of *Menges* v. *Eyster*[1] prevail to exclude it? It would seem not, for at the time that the testimony was taken the witness was competent on his own behalf, and notes of that testimony or his deposition taken at that time on his own behalf would be competent, notwithstanding the death of his adversary, and *a fortiori* ought the same testimony or deposition, taken at the instance of his adversary, to be evidence; the reasoning applicable to the cases under the act of 1865, that the deceased adversary knew just how far he could rebut the testimony, and when he can no longer do so, the survivor should not avail himself of the testimony taken at that time, does not apply here, for the survivor would himself have been competent at any rate. In point of fact the case cannot often occur, for both parties will usually testify on their own behalf if they are competent, and the notes of that testimony[2] would, of course, be competent evidence; but it is not impossible that a plaintiff should call the defendant for cross-examination, and then, as in *Hays's Appeal*,[3] the defendant should die before any evidence for the defence has been put in: in that case it might be a question of great importance to his executor to get the benefit of his previous testimony given under cross-examination.

But again, suppose in "an action by or against an executor," etc., a party otherwise incompetent has been called, or his deposition taken by the adverse party under the second section, and

---

[1] 35 Leg. Int., 421; *ante*, p. 77.   [2] *Ante*, p. 144.
[3] 10 N., 265; *ante*, p. 146.

not used, can he subsequently offer it on his own behalf? In this case neither party would have been competent to testify for himself, and under the authority of *Forrester* v. *Kline*[1] it would seem that his testimony, taken at that time, would be incompetent. Whether or not he could himself testify upon proof of having been previously called by the adverse party, as was ruled by that case with respect to the act of 1865, depends upon the degree of credibility which it may be held that such a call confers.[2]

[1] *Ante*, p. 76.   [2] *Ante*, p. 142.

CHAPTER VIII.

SUBSEQUENT LEGISLATION.

The Act of March 4th, 1870.—Almost contemporaneously with the passage of the act rendering parties competent to testify as to transactions subsequent to the death of the person whose estate, through a legal representative, is a party to the record, was passed another supplement to the act of 1869, to wit, the act of March 4th, 1870.[1] It is as follows:

"**The provisions of the said act, allowing any party or person to be a witness in any civil proceeding, are hereby extended so as to allow the testimony of either husband or wife to be given in his or her own behalf in any proceeding for a divorce, in every case where personal service of the subpœna is made on the opposite party, or said party appears and defends.**"

No advantage can be taken of this act unless, as it requires, personal service of the subpœna has been made on the respondent, or said party has appeared and defended.[2] Whether the mere entry of an appearance without further prosecution of the defence is sufficient has not been decided, but since the evident intent of the act is to secure personal notice of the proceedings having been given to the respondent, and the entry of an appearance on his or her behalf is evidence of this, it would seem more than probable that the mention of the second act is rather descriptive of the first than an additional prerequisite, as though the act had said "appears to defend," or "for the purpose of defending."

It was said in some of the earlier cases in the lower courts that a

---

[1] Purdon's Dig., 625, pl. 19, P. L., 36.

[2] Ramsey v. Ramsey, 5 Leg. Gaz., 53 (Feb., 1873); S. C., 1 Leg. Chron. Reps., 55.

divorce would not be granted upon the unsupported testimony of either party taken under this act,[1] but this view was repudiated in *Flattery* v. *Flattery*, 7 N., 27 (36 Leg. Int., 338, November, 1878), in which the libellant had gained a verdict from the jury, but the court reserved defendant's point that "the uncorroborated testimony of the libellant is not sufficient evidence to justify the jury in returning a verdict for libellant." Judgment was subsequently entered for the libellant, however, and on writ of error this was sustained, the court saying, in a PER CURIAM: "The law has made the libellant a competent witness. Whether credible was a question for the jury and not for the court. That she was flatly contradicted by her husband did not take the case away from the jury, is clear. It may be that the credibility of the wife, and the want of credibility of the husband, were as clear to the minds of the jury as the light of noonday. On what principle then shall we say, though the law has made her competent, and has carried her testimony into the jury-box, she was not to be believed, and that the testimony was legally insufficient?"

Competency of the Surviving Party.—The question of the competency of the survivor of either party, of course, cannot arise in the progress of a pending suit for divorce, but it has arisen in proceedings to set aside a decree of divorce, in *Fidelity Company's Appeal*, 8 W. N. C., 395 (March, 1880). In this case a decree of divorce *a. v. m.* had been made in 1865 upon the application of the husband, who died in 1877. Shortly after his death the respondent filed a petition, praying that the decree might be set aside; in its support the petitioner's deposition was taken. YERKES, J., said: "Her husband being dead she is certainly within the spirit of the exceptions of the act of 1869, and again, as at that time she was not a competent witness, she cannot be heard now to impeach the propriety of a divorce granted when her evidence would not

---

[1] Winter *v.* Winter, 7 Ph., 369; Stevenson *v.* Stevenson, Id., 386; Pyle *v.* Pyle, 30 Leg. Int., 208; S. C., 5 Leg. Gaz., 195. In the last case, however, the act was not referred to.

have been received." On other grounds, however, a conditional vacating of the decree was made, and on appeal the Supreme Court "concurred entirely in the opinion." The reason for the exclusion might have been placed also upon the more technical ground that the case was not literally within the act, which applies only to a "proceeding for a divorce" where there has been "personal service of the subpœna," or the respondent "appears and defends," none of which facts existed in this case; but the other is the broader and better ground.

The Act Purely an Enabling One.—It was said in *Bronson* v. *Bronson*, 8 Ph., 261 (C. P., 1871), that the act was to be construed purely as an enabling one, and that it conferred no authority upon the husband or wife to call the opposite party against his or her will. This, no doubt, is true; but as it has elsewhere been suggested, although this decision is usually referred to as an authority upon the construction of this act, its consideration was really unnecessary for the decision of the case.[1]

Act of June 8th, 1874, P. L., 279.[2]—As time went on the act of 1869 was seen to have many incongruities, and amongst them was that which rendered the estate of a lunatic, who, for "the purpose of giving testimony, is as good as dead," subject to the very inequality intended to be provided against by the proviso. The following act was therefore passed :

"**That so much of section one of an act, entitled 'An act allowing parties in interest to be witnesses,' approved the fifteenth day of April, Anno Domini one thousand eight hundred and sixty-nine, as provides 'that no interest nor policy of law shall exclude a party or person from being a witness in any civil proceeding,' shall not apply to actions by or against committees of lunatics, except as to matters occurring after the appointment of said committee.**"

No cases under this act seem to have arisen in the Supreme

---

[1] *Ante*, p. 140.   [2] Purdon's Digest, 1875, pl. 2.

Court.[1] It should be oberved that the right to testify after the date of the appointment is not, as it is by the act of 1870, confined to parties to the record; but interested persons, whether parties or not, are exempt from its operation as respects facts after that date.

Act of May 25th, 1878, P. L., 153.[2]—This act was passed to remedy the defects of the earlier act, made apparent by the line of cases commencing with *Hanna* v. *Wray*.[3] It is as follows:

"**That in all civil proceedings in law or equity, in any of the courts of this Commonwealth, brought by or against surviving partners, no interest or policy of law shall exclude any party to the record from testifying to matters having occurred between the surviving partners and the adverse party on the record.**"

Definition of "Partners."—Happily this act has just received interpretation upon one point, and that an important one. It was said in *Ash* v. *Guie*, 10 W. N. C., 198 (May, 1881), that the act is a remedial one, and therefore will be liberally construed so as to embrace under the term "partners" any two or more persons jointly concerned in a transaction, whether in the technical sense they are partners or not. In this case assumpsit was brought on a $100 bond against Ash and 109 other persons, alleged to have been "lately trading as Williamson Lodge, No. 309, A. Y. M." The use plaintiff was called on his own behalf; he was admitted, and the verdict and judgment being for the plaintiff the defendants took a writ of error. The judgment was reversed on other grounds, but upon this point the court, TRUNKEY, J., delivering the opinion, said: "Its spirit embraces the survivor of two or more who jointly contract. If two persons jointly execute a note, and one die, in an action between the holder and the survivor this statute should apply as if the makers had been partners.

---

[1] Kauffman *v.* Kauffman, 1 York Leg. Rec., 194 (C. P., Jan., 1881).
[2] Purdon's Digest, 2116, pl. 2.   [3] *Ante*, p. 110.

Otherwise, the mischief is only partially remedied. Those jointly concerned in a transaction are partners in the popular sense of the word, and, considering the obvious intendment of the statute, it should apply in the case of a surviving partner, in the popular as well as the technical sense."

The Act of May 11th, 1881, P. L., 20.—The decision in *Whitney* v. *Shippen*, 2 W. N. C., 470 (S. C., 8 N., 22),[1] showed another omission in the act of April 10th, 1870, which it was clear was at variance with the scheme of the preceding legislation, in restoring the competency of *parties* excluded by the proviso to the act of 1869, but not that of persons interested. This omission has been remedied at the session of the legislature just past by an act amending the act of April 9th, 1870, so as to read as follows:

"**Sec. 1.—In all actions or civil proceedings in any of the courts of this Commonwealth, brought by or against executors, administrators or guardians, or in actions where the assignor of the thing or contract in action may be dead, no interest nor policy of law shall exclude any party, or person, from testifying to matters occurring since the death of the person whose estate, through a legal representative, is a party to the record."**[2]

This is so completely a reproduction of the former act, with the exception of the addition of the two words previously omitted, that whatever may have been said with reference to the interpretation of and the practice under the one will apply to the other, should it ever become the subject of litigation.

Here ends the list of statutory enactments by which the incompetency of witnesses in civil proceedings in this State has been removed. There remain to be considered, however, a few general results growing out of this legislation, which may all be collected in a single chapter.

---

[1] *Ante*, p. 131.   [2] *Vide* Appendix for the text of the whole act.

CHAPTER IX.

GENERAL RESULTS OF THE LEGISLATION.

The Act of April 15th, 1869, an Enabling Act.—It has frequently been urged in the argument of cases arising under the act of 1869, that it introduced a new principle of exclusion, to wit, that of inequality between the parties, not known before, the effect of which would in many cases have been to make it a restraining rather than an enabling act. Whenever this argument has been advanced, however, it has been repudiated. It is true that the inequality of the parties has been made the chief ground upon which the existing incompetency has been permitted to remain;[1] from this, however, it has simply resulted that the reasons for incompetency already existing have been resolved into a somewhat different shape, but they have not been held to embrace any cases not heretofore within their scope. This was pointed out by WILLIAMS, J., in *McFerren* v. *Mont Alto Iron Company*, 26 Sm., 183 (July, 1874): "It is an enabling, and not a restraining statute; and the proviso was not intended to apply to a person competent as a witness before the passage of the act, and therefore not within its provisions;"[2] by SHARSWOOD, J., in *Sheetz* v. *Hanbest's Exrs.*, 31 Sm., 102 (March, 1876): "No person competent before the passage of the act was rendered thereafter incompetent, either by the words or the spirit of the law;" by MERCUR, J., in *Pratt* v. *Patterson*, 81 Sm., 117 (May, 1876): "It must not be overlooked that the Act of 15th April 1869 is an enlarging, not a restraining act. It makes no witness nor evidence incompetent that was competent before its passage;" by PAXSON, J., in *American Life Insurance*

---

[1] *Cf.* Menges *v.* Eyster, 35 Leg. Int., 421; Crouse *v.* Staley, 3 W. N. C., 83.

[2] The decision in this case, however, has been commented on elsewhere. *Ante*, p. 117.

and Trust Company v. *Shultz,* 1 N., 51 (May, 1876): " It was manifestly intended to enlarge, not to restrain the admission of evidence ;" and by a PER CURIAM in *Vidal's Appeal,* 7 W. N. C., 159 (February, 1879): " He was a competent witness then before the passage of the Act of April 15, 1869 (Pamph. L., 30), and it is now well settled that no person competent before the passage of that Act was thereby rendered incompetent."[1]

Whoever was competent at common law, or could have been called under the Act of March 27th, 1865, or those of March 28th or April 10th, 1867, remains equally competent to-day, notwithstanding the fact that the case may fall within the terms of the proviso : *Ash* v. *Guie,* 10 W. N. C., 198 (May, 1881).

There is but one act of all those which have since been passed which does not come within the same category as enabling legislation, that is the act of June 8th, 1874.[2]

The credibility of witnesses rendered competent by statute.

All parties and persons rendered competent witnesses by statute, are entitled to be regarded as other competent witnesses with respect to their credibility.

It has been said that *Sower* v. *Weaver,* 28 Sm., 443, was erroneously supposed to have decided that the testimony of both husband and wife was equivalent to that of but one witness.[3] This was not the meaning of the decision, nor is it the result of any of the other cases. The effect to be given to such testimony by the court must be the same precisely as that given to any other witness, while the credibility which the jury are to attach to it is to be left to them in this as in all other cases, but it is not for the court to say whether or not there is sufficient or insufficient evidence by reason of its having been furnished by witnesses hitherto incompetent.

---

[1] To the same effect, Buchanan *v.* Streper, 5 W. N. C., 289 (C. P., 4, March, 1878); *ante,* p. 41 ; see Mann *v.* Wieand, 4 W. N. C., 6 (January, 1877); Whipper's Est., 4 W. N. C., 527 (O. C., December, 1877); Perry *v.* Perry, 31 Leg. Int., 372 (Oct., 1874) ; Mulford *v.* Downer, 10 W. N. C., 446 (March, 1881).

[2] *Ante,* p. 153. [3] *Ante,* p. 93.

In *Prowattain* v. *Tindall*, 30 Sm., 295 (2 W. N. C., 265, January, 1876), covenant was brought by Tindall against Prowattain to recover the amount of a ground-rent paid off by Tindall, which Prowattain by his deed to Tindall had himself covenanted to pay off. The defendant testified that the deed was given upon the express understanding that Tindall had already paid off the ground-rent, and that he would not be liable. His testimony was entirely uncorroborated. The judge charged that his testimony must be disregarded by the jury unless corroborated by other witnesses or documentary testimony. It was said by GORDON, J., on writ of error taken by the defendant: "Such testimony, just as any other, must be submitted to the jury, and it is for that body to say how far the interest of the witnesses giving it shall affect its credibility. The jury may discard it as unworthy of belief, but the court may not so do."

In *Shaffer* v. *Clark*, 9 N., 94 (7 W. N. C., 459, May, 1879), on a *sci. fa.* to revive a judgment against Shaffer as surety on a judgment note, the defendant testified that he had given the plaintiff notice to collect, etc. This testimony was not corroborated, and was flatly contradicted by the plaintiff. In his charge the judge of the lower court had said to the jury: "There is no sufficient evidence upon which to submit to you the question of notice." There was a verdict and judgment for the plaintiff. On writ of error, taken by the defendant, this was held to be error, MERCUR, J., delivering the opinion, and relying upon the authority of *Prowattain* v. *Tindall* and *Flattery* v. *Flattery*.[1]

How far a chancellor is to be bound by the testimony of interested witnesses as against that of others has not been distinctly decided. It was said in *Ballentine* v. *White*, 27 Sm., 20 (November, 1874), by SHARSWOOD, J., on the duty of the judge acting as a chancellor in equitable ejectments: "How far he may be called on to exercise his discretion upon the credibility of witnesses

---

[1] *Ante*, p. 152.

it is not necessary to decide. That is now a very important question, since both parties are competent witnesses, and when their testimony is in direct conflict, the chancery rule may perhaps be invoked, that when the equity is distinctly denied by the defendant, his denial must prevail, unless other evidence be given than that of the plaintiff alone." The rule to be followed, which is certainly safe and in keeping with the other decisions in every case, would seem to be to treat the testimony of interested parties exactly as that of others; their manner and bearing, and, above all, the circumstances under which they testify, may indeed affect their credibility, but their testimony is entitled to be weighed with just the same care as that of any one else.

Parties to the Record.—*The policy of the law no longer excludes a party to the record from being a witness, unless he is also interested.*

In *Craig* v. *Brendel*, 19 Sm., 153 (October, 1871),[1] the point was not raised that the witness was inadmissible simply because of being a party to the record, but one reason upon which the admission was based, was the absence of interest, and upon this ground the case is still an authority. In *Williams* v. *Davis*, 19 Sm., 21 (July, 1872), ejectment was brought by Williams against Davis and wife, for land purchased by the plaintiff under a judgment against Davis; the land had previously been conveyed by Davis to his wife, and it was alleged that this was in fraud of creditors. Before the trial Davis had died, and his heirs, of whom Shadrach Davis was one, were substituted. He was held competent as a witness for the defence, because "he did not claim any interest in the property as heir of his deceased father, or otherwise, and was, therefore, not within the exception to the act." There is no intimation in the report that the witness had disclaimed in accordance with the act of March 28th, 1867;[2] it is therefore to be in-

---

[1] *Ante*, p. 116.
[2] Purdon's Dig., 624, pl. 14; *ante*, p. 81.

ferred that, since the passage of the Act of 1869, the mere fact of being a party on the record is no disqualification.

In *Simpson's Executor* v. *Bovard*, 24 Sm., 351 (January, 1874), the point was flatly decided. Judgment by confession had been entered in favor of Simpson against Campbell and Bovard, and subsequently it was opened to let Bovard into a defence; in the meantime Simpson died, and his executor was substituted as plaintiff. On the trial Campbell was called by the defendant and admitted. On writ of error, although the judgment for defendant was reversed for other reasons, as to this assignment of error the court, MERCUR, J., delivering the opinion, said: "The plaintiff being an executor, and the evidence relating to what transpired during the life of his testator, it is contended that the act of 15th April 1869 is inapplicable. Prior to this act, the general rule in Pennsylvania undoubtedly was, that a party to the record was incompetent to testify. Generally a principal debtor is not a competent witness for a surety in an action against the latter. Whenever, however, the suit is ended as to the principal, and the defence made by the surety is personal as to him, as were the facts here, the principal is substantially discharged from the record. Although no regular feigned issue be formed in practice, yet, under the order of court, the trial is in the nature of one and embraces only the parties thereto. Campbell was therefore a competent witness: Talmage et al. *v.* Burlingame *et al.*, 9 Barr, 21."

The result of this would seem to be to abrogate entirely the rule of *Swanzey* v. *Parker*, 14 Wr., 441,[1] by which the consent of all other parties to the record is made requisite to the admission of one of them as a witness, and it restores the previous rule of *Moddewell* v. *Keever*, 8 W. & S., 63, and *Solms* v. *McCulloch*, 5 B., 473,[2] that either co-plaintiffs or co-defendants are competent to testify against their fellows, if it is not in their own interest, notwithstanding the fact that the action may be one within the pro-

---

[1] *Ante*, p. 52.   [2] *Ante*, p. 56.

viso. Indeed, the reason of the rule of *Swanzey* v. *Parker* fell when the act of 1865 had rendered any plaintiff or defendant liable to be called by his adversary, and the act of 1867 had rendered co-plaintiffs and co-defendants competent in every such case.

This was again specifically decided in *Ash* v. *Guie*, 10 W. N. C., 198 (May, 1881), where, in an action against the members of an unincorporated society, sued as partners, two of the defendants were called by the plaintiff against the objection of their co-defendants, and the ruling was sustained on appeal, because they could have been called under the act of March 27th, 1865,[1] and the act of 1869 took away no privilege existing at the time of its passage.

Releases.— *Whenever interested persons wholly part with, or, by reason of a release to them, lose their interest in the action, they are competent, notwithstanding the case is not within the enabling legislation.*

In May, 1872, was decided *McClelland's Executor* v. *West's Admr.*, 20 Sm., 183 (May, 1872). It was an action of assumpsit, brought by the administrator of West, "to the use of Jacob D. West and George L. West, now for the use of Jacob D. West and Daniel F. Cooper," against the executor of McClelland. The plaintiff offered as a witness Enos West, son of the intestate, who was objected to, and thereupon he executed to George L. West a release of all his interest in the estate of his father. He was then admitted, and the verdict and judgment being for the plaintiff the defendant took a writ of error, but the judgment was affirmed, the court, AGNEW, J., delivering the opinion, saying: "The objection to the competency of Enos West as a witness cannot be sustained. . . . . Since the Act of 1869, enacting that neither interest nor policy of law shall exclude a witness, the ground of *Post v. Avery* is removed by legislation. Now the policy at the bottom of that case and its sequents is reversed, and primâ facie all witnesses are competent so far as interest and policy are in the

---

[1] *Ante*, p. 74.

question. It therefore lay upon the defendant to show a ground of incompetency still remaining to exclude the witness."¹ At the same time *Watts* v. *Leidig*, 29 Leg. Int., 293 (May, 1872), was decided, in which a release given to one who might be liable over, and who had been substantially a party to the contract on which the suit was brought, though not a party on the record, was held inoperative. The opinion of JUNKIN, P. J., in the lower court, was based upon the rule of *Graves* v. *Griffin* (7 H., 179), but no opinion was delivered upon the affirmance of the judgment, and the case was so different from *McClelland's Exr.* v. *West's Admr.*, and occurred so soon after *Karns* v. *Tanner*, where the equality of parties to the contract was made so important a feature, that it was probably not well considered on this point. Be that as it may, its authority was weakened by the dictum in the former case, and has been completely overturned by the recent decision of *Evans* v. *Jenks's Executrix*, 9 W. N. C., 139 (March, 1880). This was an action of covenant by the executrix of Jenks against Daniel Evans, as surety on a lease of William M. Evans and Simms, lessees; the plea was "covenants performed, *absque hoc.*" The defendant having called Simms as a witness he was objected to; the defendant then executed a release to him and his co-lessee, and renewed his offer, but the witness was excluded, and the verdict and judgment were for the plaintiff. On writ of error the judgment was reversed, TRUNKEY, J., who delivered the opinion, saying: "Being released by the surety from all liability to him, the principal has no interest in the action against the surety, and is competent to impeach the validity of the agreement, or to prove its satisfaction."²

These two cases are irreconcilable, and the last is undoubtedly in keeping with the decisions, which no longer exclude parties to

---

¹ To the same effect: Perry v. Perry, 31 Leg. Int., 372 (1874); Bruner v. Wallace, 8 W. N. C., 199 (C. P., 4, February, 1880),—in this case, however, the release was unnecessary.

² See also Wright v. Funk, 9 W. N. C., 249 (March, 1880).

the record as such, whether within the act or not,[1] and the final outcome of the principle is that no one of the three grounds of incompetency, said to be founded on the policy of the law alone, but really the outgrowth of the incompetency from interest, that of being a party on the record, a party to negotiable paper, or the assignor of a chose in action, any longer exists; the policy of the law now is to admit all persons as witnesses not clearly incompetent, and in accordance with this policy there has been restored the rule of *Steele* v. *Phœnix Ins. Co.*, and assignments and releases are no longer colorable because given by parties on the record.

The Effect upon other Rules of Evidence.—It was said in *Nichols* v. *Haynes*, 28 Sm., 174 (March, 1875), PER CURIAM: "Questions in relation to books of entry as evidence, since the Act of 1869, making the parties witnesses, stand upon a different footing from that on which they stood before. Then the book itself was the evidence, and the oath of the party was merely supplementary. Now the party himself is a competent witness, and may prove his own claim as a stranger would have done before the Act of 1869. . . . . Lumping charges would not stand as evidence in a book, but the testimony of the witness that the entry was composed of items known to him to be furnished, would be competent to go to the jury. His knowledge that the sum was correct, would make it evidence, leaving the credibility of the fact to be determined by the jury."

But on the other hand, upon another point, PAXSON, J., said in *McKinney* v. *Snyder*, 28 Sm., 497 (May, 1875): "The practical working of the recent Act of Assembly, allowing the parties in a controversy to be examined as witnesses on their own behalf, admonishes us that it would be unwise to relax any of the rules of law in cases arising under the Statute of Limitations, and of Frauds and Perjuries;" and in *Railroad Co.* v. *Shay*, 1 N., 198 (June, 1876), in which fraud was charged in obtaining a release under

---

[1] Craig *v.* Brendel; Williams *v.* Davis, p. 159.

which defendants protected themselves, SHARSWOOD, J., said: "The evidence of fraud must be clear. . . . . Since parties are allowed to testify on their own behalf, it has become still more necessary that this important rule should be strictly adhered to and enforced."

Matters of Practice.—It will be remembered that all matters of practice which have any bearing upon the time and manner of bringing objections to the competency of witnesses before the court, and the character of those objections, *mutatis mutandis* apply now with the same force as they did before the passage of the acts, and many of the cases already cited upon these points arose upon objections made to witnesses as not being within the enabling legislation.

Previous Admissions of Party.—On another point of practice, however, that of contradicting a witness by evidence of previous declarations inconsistent with his testimony, it was, until recently, supposed that the position of a party was different from that of other witnesses, since it was said that in the case of parties it is unnecessary to first call his attention to admissions out of court before placing them in evidence, because they are of themselves admissible in evidence, apart from their being used to impeach his credibility: *Brubaker* v. *Taylor*, 26 Sm., 83 (May, 1874); *Kreiter* v. *Bomberger*, 1 N., 59 (May, 1876). But it has very recently been decided as settling the conflicting authorities upon this point as it respects all witnesses, that it is a matter which "rests in the sound discretion of the judge, and unless that discretion be abused its exercise is not ground for reversal:" *Rothrock* v. *Gallaher*, 10 N., 108 (October, 1879).

Continuance on Account of Absence of Party.—It was said by HARE, J., in *Brice* v. *Shultz*, 6 Ph., 264: "That the same steps must be taken to procure the testimony of a party to the cause, or procure a continuance in the event of his absence, that would be requisite in the case of any other witness."

Cross-examination of a Party testifying on his own behalf.—It is within the discretion of the court how far the cross-examination of a witness may go ;[1] but in general a defendant will not be permitted to bring out new matter as his own defence on cross-examination, and this rule, it is said, should be the more strictly observed in the case of the cross-examination of a party to the record, who may be subsequently called under the second section of the act as if for cross-examination: *Malone* v. *Dougherty*, 29 Sm., 46 (October, 1875).

[1] Jackson *v.* Litch, 12 Sm., 451.

APPENDIX.

An Act

Relating to Evidence in Actions of Ejectment.

SECTION 1. *Be it enacted by the Senate and House of Representatives of the Commonwealth of Pennsylvania in General Assembly met, and it is hereby enacted by the authority of the same,* That in all actions of ejectment against two, or more persons, any of the defendants shall be competent as a witness for either plaintiff, or defendant, as effectually as if not made a party to the record: *Provided,* That it shall appear to the court, upon the trial, that the party, so offered as a witness, has disclaimed, upon the record, all title to the premises in controversy, at the time of action brought, and paid into court the costs already accrued, or given security for the payment thereof, at the discretion of the court.

APPROVED, the twenty-seventh day of March, Anno Domini one thousand eight hundred and sixty-seven.

P. L. 47.

A Supplement

To an Act, entitled "An Act amending the Law of Evidence in Pennsylvania," approved the twenty-seventh day of March, one thousand eight hundred and sixty-five.

SECTION I. *Be it enacted by the Senate and House of Representatives of the Commonwealth of Pennsylvania in General Assembly met, and it is hereby enacted by the authority of the same,* That in all civil actions now pending, or hereafter brought, where there are more than one plaintiff, or defendant, and either party shall compel one of the adverse parties to testify, under the act to which this is a supplement, the co-plaintiff, or co-plaintiffs, or co-defendant, or co-defendants, of the party, so compelled to testify, shall also be allowed to give evidence.

APPROVED, the tenth day of April, Anno Domini one thousand eight hundred and sixty-seven.

P. L. 60.

An Act

To amend an Act, entitled "A Supplement to an Act, entitled 'An Act Allowing Parties in Interest to be Witnesses.'"

SECTION 1. *Be it enacted, etc.*, That the act, approved ninth April, one thousand eight hundred and seventy, entitled "A supplement to an act, entitled 'An act allowing parties in interest to be witnesses,'" which is as follows: "In all actions or civil proceedings in any of the courts of this Commonwealth, brought by or against executors, administrators, or guardians, or in actions where the assignor of the thing or contract in action may be dead, no interest or policy of law shall exclude any party to the record from testifying to matters occurring since the death of the person whose estate, through a legal representative, is a party to the record," be amended so as to read as follows: "In all actions or civil proceedings in any of the courts of this Commonwealth, brought by or against executors, administrators, or guardians, or in actions where the assignor of the thing or contract in action may be dead, no interest or policy of law shall exclude any party, or person, from testifying to matters occurring since the death of the person whose estate, through a legal representative, is a party to the record."

APPROVED, the eleventh day of May, A.D. 1881.
P. L. 20.

INDEX.

ACTIONS.
    Definition of, under act of April 15th, 1869, 99–101
    By or against executors, administrators, or guardians, 101–107
    Where the assignor of the thing or contract in action is dead; 107–130

ADMINISTRATOR.
    When competent in his own favor, 37
    To prove his intestate's books, 42
        Ground therefor, 43
    Incompetency of, removed by act of March 27th, 1865, 73–74
    Application of proviso to act of April 15th, 1869, 101–106
    Extent to which exclusion under proviso operates, 115, 124
    Not to be regarded as an "assignor," 123
    In actions by or against, testimony of all facts subsequent to death competent, 131
    The exception to the proviso to the act of April 15th, 1869, considered, 133

ADVERSE PARTY.
    May be called as a witness under act of March 27th, 1865, 74
    Deposition or testimony, effect of taking under act of March 27th, 1865, 75, 76
    Definition of under act of March 27th, 1865, 79–80
    May be called for cross examination under act of April 15th, 1869, 138
        Effect of calling for cross-examination, 138
        Who may be called, 139
        Not to be called before trial without affidavit, 144

AFFIDAVIT.
    Of party, when admissible at common law, 41
    Necessary to be filed, before calling adverse party for cross-examination, 144

AGENT.
    When principal incompetent to prove himself an, 31
    What is his interest in the record, 35
    Incompetent when his own negligence is point at issue, 35, 45
        Not otherwise, 36, 46
    Fiduciary, when incompetent, 36
    Exception to rule of incompetency in case of, 44–46
    Deputy of, not incompetent, 45

ASSIGNOR.
Of fund or property, when incompetent, 25, 28, 33
Of chose in action, incompetency of, on implied warranty, 34
    Development of reason for incompetency of, 52
    Total removal of incompetency, 163
Of thing or contract in action discussed, 107–130
    Definition of, 107, 114, 120
    Must have been beneficially interested, 121
    Testimony of all facts subsequent to death of, competent, 131
    Exception to the proviso of the act of April 15th, 1869, 133

ATHEIST.
Subject to general incompetency, 18

ATTORNEY.
Competent for client, 45
Negligence of, not presumed, 46
Confidential communications of client to, protected, 18, 87, 98

AUDITOR.
Report of, effect of admission of incompetent witness, 65

BILLS OF EXCHANGE AND PROMISSORY NOTES.
Drawer of, when competent, 38
When liability for costs renders him incompetent, 39
Maker, when incompetent, 39
Development of rule of Walton v. Shelly, 48, 53
Abandonment of policy of exclusion of the maker or indorser of negotiable paper, 89, 163

CESTUI QUE TRUST.
Privilege of, in refusing to testify, 47
Removal of interest by release, 57

CHARGE.
Of court, character of, as to incompetent witnesses, 65

CHILDREN.
Incompetency of, 18

CO-DEFENDANTS, CO-PLAINTIFFS.
When incompetent, 56
Of parties called under act of March 27th, 1865, made competent by act of April 10th, 1867, 81
Act of April 10th, 1867, not applicable to cases within section 2, act of April 15th, 1869, 143

COMMISSION.
Testimony of witness rendered competent by act of April 15th, 1869, may be taken by, 138, 143

CONESTOGA FISHING ACT.
Prosecutions under, 70

CONFIDENTIAL COMMUNICATIONS.
Of attorney and client incompetent, 18

CONFIDENTIAL COMMUNICATIONS.
    Protected in legislation, 87, 98
    Of husband and wife incompetent, 18
        Protected by legislation, 87, 97

CONTRACT.
    Conditional, between witness and party renders him incompetent, 35
    Original parties to, incompetent, 53
    In action defined, 113

CONTRACTOR.
    When incompetent in *sci. fa.* sur mechanic's lien, 36

CORPORATION.
    Members of, when incompetent, 25, 26
    Stockholder of, when incompetent, 31
        Removal of interest of, 57
    Religious and charitable, exception to rule of incompetency of members, 46

COSTS.
    Liability for, ground for exclusion as incompetent, 23
        When this arises, 23, 24
    When it determines preponderance of interest, 38, 39
    Payment of past and prospective, necessary for release, 58

COURT.
    Must determine competency, 61
    But not facts, 62
    Rulings of, presumption in favor of, 63
    Duty of, when evidence is admissible at all, 64
        In charging jury, 65
    Orphans', discretion of, under act of 1832, 72
        Settlement of estates in, 102
    Rule of, as to calling adverse party for cross-examination, 144

CREDIBILITY.
    Tendency to exchange incompetency for question of, 69
    Of adverse party, called under act of March 27th, 1865, 75
        Lost by death of party calling, 75, 76
    Of co-plaintiffs and co-defendants under act of April 10th, 1867, 81, 143
    Of husband and wife under act of April 15th, 1869, 93
    Of adverse party, called under section 2, act of April 15th, 1869, 142-3
    Of party, not secured by admission of deposition of adverse party, 147
    Of witnesses rendered competent by statute, 157

CREDITOR.
    When incompetent in suit by or against debtor, 25, 27

CROSS-EXAMINATION.
    Of party under section 2, act of April 15th, 1869, 138
        Who may be called, 139
        In divorce proceedings, 140
        In cases not within enabling legislation, 141
        Before trial regulated by rule of court, 144
        Testifying on his own behalf, 164

DEATH.

Of adverse party, effect upon credibility of witness called under act of March 27th, 1865, 75, 76
Of "assignor," etc., effect of, upon testimony of survivor, 115
    Testimony of all subsequent facts competent, 131
After, notes of testimony or deposition of competent witness admissible, 144

DEBTOR.

Competency of, in suit by or against creditors, 28
Original, when incompetent in suit against third person, 30, 31, 32
    Incompetent in suit by principal against agent, 33
    In suit between creditors to prove fraud in judgment against himself, 38
    In suit by assignees against a creditor, 38
    Principal, incompetent for surety, 39

DEED.

Party not competent to prove, 43
Competent to prove loss of, 42

DEPOSITION.

Taking of, party competent to prove, 43
Taken under act of March 27th, 1865, admissibility of, 75
Of parties competent under act of April 15th, 1869, 138
Of adverse party under cross-examination, 143
Of competent witness, evidence in subsequent trial, 144
    Admission of, does not render adverse party competent, 147
Of party taken under cross-examination, how far admissible for himself, 148

DEVISAVIT VEL NON.

Issue, exception to proviso of act of April 15th, 1869, 133

DEVISEE.

See LEGATEE.

DEVOLUTION.

Title by, exception to proviso of act of April 15th, 1869, 133, 136

DIVORCE.

Proceedings in, application of section 2, act of April 15th, 1869, 140
Parties competent by act of March 4th, 1870, 151

EJECTMENT.

Defendant in, one holding title under, incompetent, 36
    Who disclaims, competent under act of March 28th, 1867, 81

ELECTION CASE.

Contested, competency of petitioner in, 44

ENABLING ACTS.

Act of April 15th, 1869, essentially an, 123, 136
Act of March 4th, 1870, an, 153

EQUITY.
>   Effect of admission of incompetent witness in, 64
>   Proceedings in, application of act of April 15th, 1869, 99

ESTOPPEL.
>   To an objection to a witness, 60

EVIDENCE.
>   How obtained, 17
>   Secondary, 43

EXCEPTIONS TO RULE OF INCOMPETENCY.
>   To prove collateral facts, 41
>   *Ex necessitate rei*, 43
>   In the case of agents, 44
>   In the case of beneficial and religious societies, 46

EXECUTOR.
>   Co-executor, when incompetent, 33
>   Under plea admitting assets incompetent, 36
>   Incompetent to sustain the will, 36
>   Incompetency removed by act of March 27th, 1865, 73–74
>   Application of act of April 15th, 1869, to case of, 101–106
>   Extent of exclusion under proviso to act of April 15th, 1869, 115, 124
>   Not to be regarded as an assignor, 123
>   In actions by or against, testimony of *all* facts subsequent to death of testator competent, 131
>   The exception to the proviso of the act of April 15th, 1869, 133

EX NECESSITATE REI.
>   How far ground for exception to rule of incompetency, 43, 44
>   Extension of rule by legislation, 70

FACT.
>   Questions of, court not bound to determine, 63
>   Upon which "objection" is based must appear, 63
>   All prior to death of "assignor," etc., excluded, 115
>   All subsequent to death competent, 131

FRAUDS, STATUTE OF.
>   Effect of enabling legislation upon rules under, 163

GUARDIAN.
>   Competency under Act March 27th, 1865, 73
>   In actions by or against, competency of parties and interested persons, 106

HEIRS.
>   When incompetent, 25, 29
>   Removal of interest of, 58

HUSBAND AND WIFE.
>   Special incompetency of, for or against each other, 19
>   >   Origin of rule, 19
>   >   Legislation in England and other states, 82, 83
>   >   For each other removed by act of April 15th, 1869, 92

176 INDEX.

HUSBAND AND WIFE.
    Against each other in divorce removed by act of March 4th, 1870, 151
    Single exception in case of wife, 44
    Proof of non-access, incompetent, 88
    Interest against either defined, 94, 97
    Confidential communications of, 18, 87, 97
    May be called by each other under section 2, act of April 15th, 1869, 140
    Wife not within definition of "adverse party," act of March 27th, 1865, 80, 140

IDENTITY.
    Of books, papers, etc., party competent to prove, 41, 42

IDIOTS.
    Subject to general incompetency, 18

IN EQUILIBRIO.
    Interest, what is, 38

INCOMPETENCY.
    Of testimony, 17
    Of witnesses, 17
        General, 17, 18
        Special, 17, 19
        Views of Lord Hardwicke and Lord Mansfield, 69
        Gradual removal of by legislation, 69
        Acts of 1865 and 1867, 73-84
        Executors, administrators, and trustees, act of March 27th, 1865, 73, 74
        Adverse party on the record, act of March 27th, 1865, 80
        Parties and interested persons, act of April 15th, 1869, and April 9th, 1870, 85-150
        In divorce, act of March 4th, 1870, 151
        In actions by or against lunatics, act of June 8th, 1874, 153
        In actions by or against surviving partners, act of May 25th, 1878, 154
        Persons in interest, act of May 11th, 1881, 155

INCOMPETENT TESTIMONY.
    Definition of, 17
    Various kinds of, 18
    Not necessary for consideration herein, 18
    Confidential communications of attorney and client protected by act of April 15th, 1869, 87, 98
    Husband and wife protected by act of April 15th, 1869, 87, 97
    Act of April 15th, 1869, does not affect, 110

INHABITANTS.
    Incompetency of, 25
        Difference between rated and ratable, 25
        Removed by legislation, 70, 71

INFAMY.
    As ground of incompetency, 18
        Removal of, 19, 91
        Effect of proviso to act of April 15th, 1869, 130
    Infamous crimes, what are, 18

INSOLVENCY.
    How far, affects competency of creditor or legatee, 27, 29

INTEREST.
    Incompetency arising from, 20
        Gilbert's reasons for, 20
        Peake's reasons for, 20
    In a suit, definition of, 21
    In the result of the issue, 23
        Liability for costs, 23
        Interest in a fund, 23
    In the record as an instrument of evidence, 29
        To shift a burden of debt, 30
        To exonerate from secondary liability, 33
        Where it may be used to sustain a claim, 35
        To fix liability on witness, 35
        Where judgment may serve to charge an estate, 37
    In equilibrio, 38
    Preponderance of, 38
    Testimony against, 39, 40
    Exceptions to rule of exclusion, 41–46
    Removal of disqualification, by release, 48–55, 57–59, 161
    Removal of disqualification by legislation, 69
        Acts of 1865 and 1867, 73–84
        Acts of 1869 and 1870, 85, 131
        Act of March 4th, 1870 (Divorce), 151
        Act of May 25th, 1878 (Partners), 154
        Act of May 11th, 1881, 155
    Act of June 8th, 1874 (Lunatics), 153

INTOXICATED PERSONS.
    Subject to general incompetency, 18

ISSUES AND INQUIRIES.
    Devisavit vel non and others, 133

JUDGMENT.
    Record of, when evidence, 29, 30

LEGATEE.
    Liability of for costs, 24
    When incompetent, 25, 29
    Preponderance of interest, 39
    Removal of interest of, 57–58

LEGISLATION.
    Early legislation, 69–72
        Subsequent acts. *See* INTEREST.

INDEX.

LIMITATIONS, STATUTE OF.
    May serve as bar to incompetency, 37
    Effect of enabling legislation upon rules under, 163

LUNATICS.
    Subject to general incompetency, 18
    Committee of, when incompetent, 32
        Actions by or against, act of June 8th, 1874, 153

MORTGAGOR.
    When incompetent, 31

NEGLIGENCE.
    Of agent, when it renders him incompetent, 35, 36, 45
    Not presumed in an attorney, 46

NEGOTIABLE PAPER.
    Drawer of, when competent, 38
        Liability for costs, ground of incompetency, 39
    Maker, when incompetent, 39
    Rule of *Walton* v. *Shelly*, 48, 53
    Abandonment of rule, 89, 163

NOTICE.
    Proof of, by party, 42

OBJECTION.
    Time of, 60
    Method of bringing before court, 61
    Character of, 63

ORIGINAL ENTRIES.
    Competency of party to prove, 42
    Effect of enabling legislation upon rule, 163

ORPHANS' COURT.
    Act of March 29th, 1832, relating to, 71
        Discretion under, 72
    Act of April 15th, 1869, applicable to proceedings in, 99
    Settlement of estates in, 102

PARTNER.
    Incompetency of, for or against firm, 25, 26
        To prove partnership, 32
        To prove payment to himself, 32
        To prove facts exonerating himself, or giving right to contribution, 32
    When privileged not to testify, 47
    Actions by or against surviving, 110, 111, 112
    Competency of parties to transactions with surviving, Act of May 25th, 1878, 154
    "Partner" defined, 154

PARTY.
    Definition of, 24

PARTY.
> Incompetency of, general rule, 20
>> Exceptions, 41–46
>> Development of rule, 48–52
>> Reasons for, 20, 51
>> Not removed by release, 51, 52, 58
>> In actions by or against executors, administrators, or guardians, 101, 106
>> Of all under proviso to act of April 15th, 1869, 124
>> To the record, no longer the policy of the law, 159
> Privilege of, in refusing to testify, 46, 47
> To negotiable paper, when incompetent, 54
>> Limitations of rule, 54, 55
>> Abandonment of rule, 163
> Examination of on *voir dire*, 62–63
> Adverse, who is under, act of March 27th, 1865, 79
>> Cross-examination of, act of April 15th, 1869, section 2, 138
>>> Who may be called, 139
> To a transaction, not *ipso facto* an "assignor," 123
>> With surviving partner competent, act of May 25th, 1878, 154
> Absence of, continuance on account of, 164
> Testifying on his own behalf, cross-examination of, 164

POLICY OF LAW.
> Defined, 88–91
> No longer excludes party to record, 159
> As ground for exclusion abandoned, 163

PRACTICE.
> Time of objection to witness, 60
> Method of bringing objection before the court, 61
> Character of objection, 63
> Court to determine competency, 62
>> But not questions of fact, 63
> Competency of witness for one point and not another, 64
> Effect of admission of incompetent witness in equity, 64
> Charge of court on question of competency, 65
> Rule of court as to cross-examination of adverse party, 144
> No change in by legislation, 164
> Evidence of previous admissions of party, 164
> Continuance on account of absence of, 164
> Cross-examination of party testifying on his own behalf, 165

PREPONDERANCE.
> Of interest, what is, 38
> Of interest of adverse party on the record, 80

PRINCIPAL.
> Apparent, when incompetent to prove himself agent, 31, 45, 46

PRIVILEGE.
> Of refusing to testify when it exists, 46, 47
>> Removed by act of March 27th, 1865, 74
> Decides who is an "adverse party," 79

PURCHASER.
    When incompetent, 31, 37

RECORD.
    As an instrument of evidence, 29
    Must show error to entitle to reversal, 63

RELEASE.
    History of releases, 48–55
    Of interested person, 57
    Requisites of, 59
    Validity since act of April 15th, 1869, 161

REMOVAL OF DISQUALIFICATION.
    Of infamy by pardon and serving sentence, 19
    Of party to suit, 48–51, 161–163
    Of interest by release, 57–59, 161–163

RULE OF COURT.
    Amendment as to cross-examination of party, 144

SECONDARY EVIDENCE.
    What is, 43
    Ground for admission of, 43

SHERIFF.
    When incompetent to prove signature to bail bond, 37

SOCIETIES.
    Unincorporated, when members incompetent, 25, 26
    Trustees of beneficial, charitable, or religious competent, 46
    Members of beneficial, charitable, or religious, when incompetent, 46

SPOLIATION.
    In cases of, how far party competent, 44

STOLEN GOODS.
    Owner of made competent, 70

SURETY.
    When incompetent, 34

TENANT.
    Terre-tenant, when incompetent, 37
    Relation of landlord and, not always ground of exclusion, 37
    In common, when competent, 37
    Incompetency of, by reason of liability for costs, 39

TESTIMONY.
    Incompetent, defined, 17
    Notes of, competency in subsequent suit, 144
        Admission does not render adverse party competent, 147
        Taken under cross-examination, admission of, 148

THING IN ACTION.
    Definition of, 113

INDEX.

TIME.
    Lapse of, bar to incompetency, 37
    For objecting to competency, 60

TRESPASSERS.
    Joint, competent for either side, 32

TRUSTEES.
    Of charitable and religious societies competent, 46
    Rendered competent in their own suits, act of March 27th, 1865, 73
    Who are within act of March 27th, 1865, 74

VENDEE.
    Of land, when incompetent, 31

VENDOR.
    With warranty, when incompetent, 33
    Without warranty, or with general warranty, when competent, 33, 95
    Trustee as, competency of, 34
    Of personal property, 34, 95
    Interest of, when in equilibrio, 38
    Of land rendered competent by release, 49

VOIR DIRE.
    Examination under, to prove incompetency, 62–63

WAIVER.
    Of privilege by party, 56
    Of disqualification, 56
    Of objection to incompetency under proviso to act of April 15th, 1869, 125

WIFE.
    Special incompetency of, origin of, 19
        Exception in case of spoliation, 44
        Removed by act of April 15th, 1869, 92
        Under proviso to act of April 15th, 1869, 126
        As to facts subsequent to death of assignor under act of April 9th, 1870, 130
        Removed in divorce proceedings, act of March 4th, 1870, 151
    Not "adverse party" within act of March 27th, 1865, 80
        Nor act of April 15th, 1869, section 2, 140
    Interest against defined, 94–96
    Confidential communications of, 18, 87, 97
    Liable to be called for cross-examination in divorce proceedings, 140

WITNESS.
    Incompetency of, 17
    Competent as to some facts and not others, 64
    Incompetent, admission of, in equity, 64
    Incompetent, admission of, before auditor, 65
    Incompetent, admission of, duty of court upon, 65